A PASSION FOR CHRIST

The Vision that Ignites Ministry

Thomas F. Torrance
James B. Torrance
David W. Torrance

edited by
Gerrit Dawson
Jock Stein

THE HANDSEL PRESS
Edinburgh

PLC PUBLICATIONS
Lenoir

Joint © Handsel Press 1999 and PLC Publications 1999

British Library Cataloguing in Publication Data
A catalogue record for this publication is available from the British Library

ISBN
1 871828 49 X (Britain)
0-9652602-4-0 (USA)

Typeset in 11 pt. Garamond
at the Stables, Carberry

Printed by PrintSystems, Inc.

Cover design by John McWilliam

CONTENTS

Introduction
The Light of the Gospel   *Gerrit Dawson*   1

Chapter One
The Christ who Loves us   *Thomas F. Torrance*   9

Chapter Two
Preaching Jesus Christ   *Thomas F. Torrance*   23

Chapter Three
Christ in our Place: the Joy of Worship   *James B. Torrance*   35

Hymn
I Know Not How to Pray   *James B. Torrance*   53

Chapter Four
Prayer and the Priesthood of Christ   *James B. Torrance*   55

Chapter Five
Sharing in the Ministry of Christ   *David W. Torrance*   71

Chapter Six
Marriage in the Covenant of Christ   *David W. Torrance*   91

Chapter Seven
The Mission of Christians and Jews   *David W. Torrance*   115

Postscript
The Legacy of the Gospel   *Jock Stein*   131

Selected Books   151

Notes and Acknowledgments

The Editors express their thanks to Bob Mills and the staff of the Presbyterian Lay Committee for assistance with this publication, and especially to the Torrance brothers themselves for the use of their material.

Unless otherwise noted, Scripture references are taken from the Holy Bible, New International Version, © 1973, 1978, 1984 by the International Bible Society. Used by permision of Zondervan Publishing House. All rights reserved.

No uniform policy of capitalisation has been adopted in this book.

Introduction by Gerrit Dawson
THE LIGHT OF THE GOSPEL

From the moment I was re-introduced to the work of the Torrance brothers several years ago, something ignited in my soul. As I read, I felt like I held gold in my hands. Simultaneously, a hunger awoke and was satisfied. Ever was I directed to see a God higher and more wonderful than I had dared to imagine. Jesus Christ appeared to me through their words in the splendour of his glory and his all-embracing love. I was thrilled again with theology. Suddenly, doctrine mattered immensely, because it offered a path, not into esoteric musings, but into the very heart of the universe.

So I introduce these essays to you with earnest anticipation. I believe they will fire up your passion for Jesus Christ. For they contain the truths that keep Christian faith vigorous. As you read, you may well feel, as I did, that you are seeing something very familiar as if for the first time. The Gospel will shine with a new brilliance. For the doctrines of grace articulated in these pages take hold of us and do not let go. We may wrestle with them all night long, as Jacob with the angel, but in the morning we will be changed. Our very lives will be reoriented by the blessing of seeing anew what it means that God has come to us in Jesus Christ. Such theology is a tonic for weariness to those who are labouring in the Church. And it offers us all an opportunity to recover our confidence as we proclaim the Gospel for a new millennium.

The Present Need

The Church in the west is drowning. The tidal rush of a secular culture has long ago washed away the fortress that was Christendom. We no longer speak with authority, nor anything like a unified voice, and what whispers we do utter to our age are lost in the roar of its media sea. Prosperity unimaginable in earlier years has come to the west and to its Christians. But the very mass of our wealth threatens to push us under. We have all the resources for a vigorous Church: books, buildings, education, and enormous technology for communication. But like the culture, we are swept along by the power of a consumerist age. We can't seem to find our feet.

If we could brace ourselves against the Rock, of course, the Church could rise against the tide, speaking the words of truth and shining the light of Christ's love to those who are adrift. But far too often, we have built our ministries upon shifting sand. We have allowed the issues of the moment to undermine us.

Jesus' question remains the supreme concern of the Church in every age, 'Who do you say that I am?' And Peter's answer is the word we must speak, freshly and vitally to each generation: 'You are the Christ, the Son of the Living God.' Such bedrock, deceptively simple truth eludes us, however, while we are captivated by a pair of questions from the culture that are now assaulting the mainstream Church. The first is whether the Christ of the Gospels and the creeds is really the Jesus who lived in history. The second is the problem of the inclusive love of God and the exclusive claims of truth in Christianity. We have to find bold, credible answers to these questions if we are to recover our vision and voice for the new century.

The Real Jesus

The first question concerns our confidence that the Jesus presented to us by the Gospels, 'the Christ, the Son of the living God,' is really the Jesus who lived in Palestine two thousand years ago. Is the Christ enshrined in our creeds and confessions really anything like Jesus of Nazareth? Or, can we find the 'true Christ' who has been hidden for centuries under the agenda of the Church? The Church today is under increasing influence of those who would attempt to disentangle the 'real' Jesus from the Gospels.

Far more than just the extremes of the Jesus Seminar have been raising these issues. For years now, our mainstream seminaries and colleges have been graduating ministers who have no confidence in the texts of Scripture they are to preach. Our historical-critical methods have deconstructed the texts but we have failed to put them, and our students, back together again. These new pastors leave seminary unsure of what Jesus said and did, and suspicious of the epistles which reflect on the theological meaning of the Jesus presented in the Gospels. They have been saturated with trendy re-interpretations but parched for an in-depth knowledge of our heritage.

This ignorance has opened the way for ancient heresies to return with new vigour in the Church. Many contemporary ministers and Christians function with an Adoptionist Christology. That is to say, we read and hear that Jesus was a man who connected with God so deeply and lived so authentically that he has been called the Son of God. He wasn't really God incarnate. Rather, Jesus the man discovered 'the divine within' and related to it deeply. He is now an example and guide of what we can be in ourselves.

When such Christology is paired with the search for a Christ behind the Gospels, we are left with a Jesus, and a God, who are ultimately unknowable. Hence, we are back to ancient Gnosticism where only the expert few have enough knowledge to disentangle the texts, read the clues and tell us who Jesus is. Of course, the results of such inquiries have too often offered a Jesus strikingly similar to the interests and ideologies of the inquirers. So, distressingly too often, we have proclaimed Jesus as a mere man.

Such a view of Jesus can keep us comfortable in our culture. We can relate to the spirituality of the age, and remain safe in ourselves from the claims on us of God in Christ. But it will sink the Church and leave desperate people to drown with us. We have to recover a theology that will invigorate us to preach the truth about who Jesus is.

The Scandal of Particularity

The second question is similar. How do we reconcile the exclusive claims of Christianity with our belief in the inclusive love of God? The concern is urgent in a culture where religious pluralism is a fact. People think and believe and worship in many different ways. Our culture, however, has urged us not to compare different beliefs for truth but to affirm the validity of any belief. We are urged to celebrate diversity at the expense of making any claims to truth. Religious matters are private, and not a matter of public inquiry or marketplace debate. This, of course, ensures that the West's true dominant worldview - consumerist materialism - remains masked and in control of most of our decisions.

By contrast, the particularity of Christianity is an offence. The very idea that God would reveal himself uniquely through incarnating in one historical individual is a scandal. The question is immediately on our lips, 'But what about...' and we go on to name loved ones, friends, religions and ideas that are different than our own. It just sticks in our throats to consider that if one way is right, then the others are wrong - dangerously, perilously wrong.

God loves everyone. Jesus Christ died for everyone. How, then, can we make judgements about others?

To avoid this offence, many western Christians have adopted the culture's slogan that we are 'people of faith.' Faith in whom is not the issue - that kind of particularity is grating. Rather, what matters in our age is simply having faith in something, perhaps in yourself, or even faith in 'faith'. This benign approach offends no one at the time, but ultimately leaves people lost in themselves. The Church has to learn how to say 'You are the Christ, the Son of the Living God' in this present generation.

Of course we must say it in a way that reflects God's love. We don't want to pound the uniqueness of Christ in a threatening way. Yet our desire to avoid triumphalism and be gentle has left us not knowing how to say 'No' to the ever widening band of behaviours and ideas that are clamouring for 'inclusive' acceptance in the Church. Until we solve the exclusive\inclusive dilemma, our energy and confidence will continue to drain away. Our Church will be built on sand that washes away in the flood of culture.

Recently, a colleague of mine lamented, 'I realised I have spent most of my ministry trying to help people feel comfortable amidst the challenges to the lives they have chosen. I have failed to call them out to new lives transformed in Christ'. He, like so many of our pastors, has grown weary from working in his own strength with a watered-down, accommodating Gospel. His life and ministry revived, however, when he recovered his confidence in the clarity of the Biblical declaration of who Jesus is.

For, the Gospel is still the Gospel: the power of God for the salvation of everyone who believes. And the Church may yet get our feet planted on the Rock and begin to stand against the waves of the culture. We may yet hold out lines of rescue to God's little ones who have lost their way. But we will need a daring theology to do so.

This is what the Torrance brothers have given the Church. They speak a daring, vital word that springs first from Scripture, then rises through the great patristic writers, the creeds, the Reformers, and the evangelical theologians who have followed. Like many great theologians, the Torrances have spoken not only to their generation, but also to the one coming up. Though the brothers are past three score and ten, their words remain young in the best sense: supple, strong and vigorous for the present moment. Before turning to the essays themselves, let us briefly consider two distinctive features you may anticipate reading in all their work which reply to these two critical questions facing the western Church.

The Oneness of Jesus with the Father

It takes a bold faith to say directly, 'There is no God except the God who has come and meets us in Jesus.' This unbroken oneness between Jesus and the Father fairly sings through the theology of the Torrances. They affirm over and over that in Jesus we have revealed nothing less than who God is, both in himself and toward us. Jesus was no mere man. He was, and is, very God in our midst.

'When we look into the face of Jesus Christ and see there the very face of God,' writes Thomas Torrance, 'We know we have not seen and cannot see God anywhere else or in any other way but in him, for he is God himself come among us.' That Jesus is the supreme revelation of God necessarily judges all other knowledge of God as inferior, as but seeing through a glass darkly in comparison. This creates judgement upon any notions of God we may hold that fall outside the biblical witness to Christ. But as bracing as that reality is, it is ultimately the best possible news. Because, this means that in Jesus, 'we human beings may really and joyfully know God in his divine nature.'

Thus in Christ, the Torrances tell us, God 'refused to be alone or without us, but insisted on penetrating into the heart of our sin and violence and unappeasable agony in order to take it all upon himself and to save us.' Jesus is the exclusive, unique revelation of God. This news is joy beyond hope! God is like Jesus, and so we may be saved. God is the way Jesus is, and so we are not left alone in our lostness. God and Jesus are one, and so Jesus is 'the very heart of God Almighty beating with the pulse of his infinite love within the depth of our lost humanity in order to vanquish and do away with everything that separates us from God.'

The answer to the question posed to the Church about who is the real Jesus is emphatically answered by the Torrances. The real Jesus is God incarnate, and he is 'mediated to us in the Holy Scriptures.' The New Testament bears witness to this revelation in such a way that we are lifted into realms of thought and understanding beyond anything we might create on our own. It is not behind the texts, but through the texts that Christ comes to us. For the Torrances, there can be no tearing apart of the historical Jesus from the theological Christ. The Scriptures are to be interpreted holistically. Through the words of the New Testament, the Holy Spirit reveals to us Jesus. So, throughout the essays in this book, we discover a great love and reverence for the Scriptures: see, for example, the lovely cascade of Scriptural portrayals of Jesus in David Torrance's essay on 'Sharing in the Ministry of Christ'.

Our culture asks the Church 'Who is Jesus?' The Torrances answer resoundingly: he is the Christ Jesus of Scripture, God with us. In him we see the Father, and we discover in the giving of Jesus' life for us that 'God loves us even more than he loves himself'.

The Vicarious Humanity of Christ

The complement to the oneness in being between the Father and the Son is the oneness of the Son with our humanity. Jesus was, and is, fully human, bone of our bone and flesh of our flesh. Jesus lived in solidarity with the human race, and by fully assuming human being, he has embraced every one of us with his love. This is the doctrine of the vicarious humanity of Christ. What he was in himself as a particular human being, he was on behalf of every human being. Thus, when I am united to Christ, I am given to participate in his humanity, in all its sinless obedience, outreaching love and perfect communion with God.

So, the exclusive nature of the revelation of God in Christ, which the Church may never compromise, preserves the most inclusive love of God possible. I can hear the passion in James Torrance's voice whenever he speaks of 'the all-inclusive humanity of Christ'. Christ takes what is ours and gives us what is his. In this 'wonderful exchange', Christ assumes our place and gives us his place. He takes to himself our sin, our brokenness, our anxiety, our alienation from the Father, and our sentence of condemnation. In return, he gives to us his righteousness, his wholeness, his peace, his oneness with the Father and his declaration of eternal life. Our humanity is restored in the humanity of Christ. One on behalf of the many, he has taken the human condition to the cross, died with it and then been raised in new life, the life of a restored humanity.

Now, at the right hand of the Father, Jesus continues in this work. He continues to take our feeble prayers and make them his own. He continues to offer on our behalf even the very response to this grace which we should make but cannot ever adequately offer. He stands in for us even now. For the humanity of Christ continues. He is still God incarnate, even in his glorified life in heaven. Like his oneness with his Father, Jesus Christ's oneness with our humanity 'is a final reality enduring endlessly into eternity'.

This electrifying concept of the continuing vicarious humanity of Jesus provides the answer to the exclusive revelation\inclusive love dilemma. Jesus is the one unique and sufficient revelation of God. But that exclusive word offers a triumphant, resounding Gospel to all people. In Jesus, our humanity has been gathered up, redeemed, and restored.

Imagine if someone found a cure for a terribly debilitating disease, an illness which heretofore could only have its symptoms managed, not its root cause cured. When once this wonderful cure became available, it would diminish the place of all the other symptom controllers. In fact, people might lose jobs and companies even go out of business. The cure would make mere salves unnecessary. Of course, those who had made their living through the old medicines might protest. And those comfortable with the old ways of managing the pain might be resistant to change. But all of this would pale in comparison to the new reality: the disease has been cured! And imagine further if this wonderful treatment could be made available to all people world-wide without discrimination. The exclusive nature of its curative power would be an all inclusive joy for humankind.

This illustration is a shadow of the jubilant news of the Gospel. Jesus Christ who is God has laid hold of our humanity, so taking it into himself, that he returns it to us restored beyond its original condition. From this astounding starting point, the rest of the life of the Church unfolds. The human role is to participate now in the life of Christ Jesus in his relationship as the God\Human with his Father. As you read the following essays, you will see how the truth of who Jesus is works out in our preaching, our worship, our ministry, our prayer life, even our relationships with the people of Israel and our own families.

The Torrances' descriptions of what the incarnation really means for us, in language that is often theological poetry, create a passion for Christ. Here is a lifeline to the Rock for a drifting, drowning Church. Here are answers to the difficult questions of the hour. The Triune God of Grace is presented with urgent clarity. Personally, their thought has changed my life and re-energised my ministry. I believe that as you read, your life and ministry will be ignited in a bright flame of faith as well.

Ignition Points

What the Father is and does, Jesus is and does. And what Jesus is and does, the Father is and does. There is in fact no God behind the back of Jesus, no act of God other than the act of Jesus, no God but the God we see and meet in him.

Jesus Christ is the open heart of God, the very love and life of God poured out to redeem humankind, the mighty hand and power of God stretched out to heal and save sinners.

The ultimate destiny of humanity is bound up with Jesus Christ, for it is he who has come to invade and destroy the barrier of death and all that separates men and women from God.

Jesus Christ [is] God himself incarnate, who refused to be alone or without us, but insisted on penetrating into the heart of our sin and violence and unappeasable agony in order to take it all upon himself and to save us...

The love of the Lord Jesus in giving himself for us on the Cross for our salvation, where the infinite sacrifice of the Father and the infinite sacrifice of the Son are for ever bound up indivisibly together, assures us that the eternal God, let it be repeated, loves us more than he loves himself. God loves us with an infinite love from which nothing in life or death can ever separate us. That is the love incarnate in the Lord Jesus.

Chapter One

THE CHRIST
WHO LOVES US

Thomas F. Torrance

There is theological music in this essay to set the soul singing.
Thomas Torrance considers the reality that the Christ whom
we love is fully one with God the Father. We are introduced
to the word *homoousios*, which is Greek for 'of the same
being'. Jesus and the Father are *homoousios*, of one being
with each other. Therefore 'God is not one thing in Christ
and another thing in himself'. This has profound implications
for us. Among them is the astonishing news that God 'loves
us more than he loves himself!'

The most outstanding feature of the Gospels is their presentation
of the oneness of Jesus and his Father. The consciousness that Jesus
had of himself, and the absorbing consciousness he had of God,
were inextricably bound up together. This is particularly evident
in that supreme statement of Jesus, once called 'the most important
for Christology in the New Testament' by H.R. Mackintosh: 'I
praise you, Father, Lord of heaven and earth, because you have
hidden these things from the wise and learned and revealed them
to little children. Yes, Father, for this was your good pleasure. All
things have been committed to me by my Father. No one knows
the Son except the Father, and no one knows the Father except the
Son, and those to whom the Son chooses to reveal him' (Matt 11:25-
27). That statement is of supreme importance for our understanding
of who he was.

Then Jesus added to them the wonderful words, of no less importance for our understanding of his mission: 'Come to me, all you who are weary and burdened, and I will give you rest. Take my yoke upon you and learn from me, for I am gentle and humble in heart, and you will find rest for your souls. For my yoke is easy and my burden is light.' (Matt 11:28-30). The Person of Jesus and his mission are together grounded in and flow from his unique relation to God: God and I, I and God, the incarnate I AM of the one Lord God of heaven and earth. That is who Jesus is, as the Son of Man, the Son of God become human, the very Light, Life and Love of God Almighty. It is upon that Person as the only-begotten Son of the Father in his unqualified relation in being and doing with him that the actual import of the Gospel of God's saving love, and indeed of everything in the relation between God and humanity, humanity and God, turns.

Without that profound correlation in person and mission between God and man, Jesus would have nothing to do with any self-giving or self-revealing on the part of the eternal God, in which event the whole message of the Gospel would disappear, and the inner structure of the Christian faith would disintegrate and collapse. How then are we to understand the relation of Jesus and his mission to God? Was it merely some kind of 'moral' relation, or was there a real togetherness and oneness in being between Jesus and God, between the incarnate Son and the Father?

The Oneness Between Jesus and God

That was undoubtedly the fundamental question that faced the disciples, in which they found themselves impelled to affirm the truth of a oneness in being between Jesus and God, particularly evident in the statements of the Lord Jesus cited in the Fourth Gospel: 'I and the Father are one' (John 10:30), 'Anyone who has seen me, has seen the Father' (John 14:9). It was in accordance with such a supreme conviction that the disciples and apostles of Jesus affirmed their witness to him and composed the Gospels and the Epistles handed down to us in the Scriptures of the New Testament. The disciples and apostles realised that without a real oneness in being and act in Jesus between him and the Father, the life, teaching and mission of Jesus would have little significance for them - his identity would have had nothing to do with any self-giving or self-revealing on the part of the eternal God, and there would be no actual mediation of God through him to humankind.

That was the supreme truth, the togetherness and oneness in being and act between Jesus Christ and God, between the Son, and indeed the incarnate Son, and the Father, to which the early Church gave primary place in its belief from the very beginning. They relied on it in all acts of worship and mission, for it integrated their understanding of the apostolic and evangelical faith, and gave illuminating focus to the whole New Testament revelation of the Lord Jesus as the Light, Life and Love of God.

Before long the Church gave careful thought and precise theological expression to this all-important oneness in being between the incarnate Son and God the Father, confessing their faith in the Lord Jesus as God from God, Light from Light, true God from true God. They believed that, although Jesus Christ was truly Man born of the Virgin Mary and crucified under Pontius Pilate, he shared the same Nature and Being with God the Father, and so the Church gave decisive expression to that belief in the heart of the Nicene Creed, the supreme Creed of Christianity.

The precise theological term they used for that oneness and togetherness in being of the Lord Jesus with God the Father was the Greek expression *homoousios* (of the same being). They realised that without that mutual togetherness and oneness in being and act between the incarnate Son and the Father, the Gospel message would be empty of saving significance for humanity. Then the identity of Jesus Christ would have nothing to do with any self-giving or self-revealing on the part of the God the Father, there would be no Mediator between God and humanity, and so no substance to the Christian Gospel.

The Oneness of Father and Son: In the Life of Christ

How are we to think of this oneness in being, or unqualified correlation, between Jesus and God? What does it mean for our understanding of the Gospels and Epistles of the New Testament Scriptures today, and what they have to say to us about the salvation of humankind? To clarify that, let us ask the question: What would happen to the import of the Gospel if the relation between Jesus Christ and God the Father were not of the oneness of being affirmed by the Nicene Creed? This ought to make clear to us whether we are concerned here with the real essence of the Gospel and the heart of the Christian faith or not.

Let us consider the saving acts of Christ as we read of him and meet him in the evangelical accounts of his work of healing and forgiveness. Throughout the apostolic tradition, in the Epistles as well as in the Gospels, Jesus is presented to us as acting out of an unbroken oneness between himself and the Father, which is the very ground of his significance. In his miraculous deeds he continues the divine work of creation, and in his forgiveness of sins he exercises a prerogative that belongs to God alone. He and the Father are one in their work of healing and forgiving. That is why Jesus' acts are saving acts, for they are divine acts.

Suppose, then, that there were no such oneness in being and agency between Jesus and God: that would mean that whether in healing someone's body or in claiming to forgive sins, Jesus was acting merely on his own as another creaturely being, and acting on others only externally like a human physician, without any creative penetration into the inner condition of their need which would recreate them from within and undo the sin and guilt lodged in the depths of their existence. Separate Jesus Christ from God like that, and the saving essence goes out of the Gospel. The word of forgiveness becomes merely the word of a man, no more than an evanescent linguistic event without saving power or enduring reality, and is something entirely different from the stupendous divine act of undoing sin and recreating human being. A 'forgiveness' of that sort has no divine substance to it, for it is not backed up by the Word and Being of God himself, and lacks any kind of genuine reality, let alone any ultimate validity.

Nor does it help matters, as some heretical people thought in the Early Church, to say that Jesus Christ was 'like' God, similar in being or in nature to him. For the only kind of similarity that could give saving substance to the words and deeds of Christ would be one in which he was really like God in being and nature, and that would mean being really equal with God and of the same nature as God. That is precisely what the Nicene statement about oneness in being with God the Father was intended to declare. He only can truly and perfectly reveal God who himself is the one whom he reveals - that is what and who Jesus Christ was and is, one in person and being with God.

When we look into the face of Jesus Christ and see there the very face of God, we know we have not seen and cannot see God anywhere else or in any other way but in him, for he is God himself become human, and there is no God except the God who has come and meets us in Jesus. Who and what God really is could not be revealed to us or known by us except in and through the Incarnation. 'No one has ever seen God; the only Son, who is in the bosom of the Father, he has made him known' (John 1:18, RSV). As we learn from Jesus himself, he who has seen Jesus, has seen the Father, for he is in the Father and the Father is in him (John 14:9-10). And so Jesus said to his disciples, 'No one knows the Father except the Son' (Matt 11:27), and 'No one comes to the Father except through me' (John 14:6). If God the Father is ineffably in the Son, and the Son is ineffably in the Father, both in their distinction as Father of the Son and Son of the Father, one and the same divine Being, then it is in Jesus the incarnate Son of the Father that we human beings may really and joyfully know God in his divine nature.

The Oneness of the Father and the Son:
In The Passion of Christ

All this applies even more acutely to the passion of Christ, in which, as he claimed, he gave himself for the redemption of humankind, for his passion was also the very passion of God himself incarnate in him. What would become of our understanding of the Cross if at that supreme point Christ remained ultimately separate from God in being and nature: Christ a mere man on the Cross and God wholly other and alone in his Deity? It would then be impossible for us to believe either in God or in humanity. We could not believe in such a God who did not lift a finger to save the finest man who ever emerged in the human race. Nor could we believe in a humanity which in the face of such perfection and love in Jesus rose up, spat in his face and hounded him to death on a Roman gibbet.

To think of God only in heaven and of Jesus only a man on the Cross, leaves us in utter darkness and despair. But put God on the Cross, let Jesus Christ be God himself incarnate, who refused to be alone or without us, but insisted on penetrating into the heart of our sin and violence and unappeasable agony in order to take it all upon himself and to save us, and the whole picture is transformed. Then Jesus Christ, even in the midst of our death which he made

his own, even, even in the midst of our betrayal of him, is the very
Word and Hand of God stretched out to save us, the very heart of
God Almighty beating with the pulse of his infinite love within
the depth of our lost humanity in order to vanquish and do away
with everything that separates us from God. That is the saving
import of the togetherness and oneness in being between God the
Father and his only begotten Son - apart from it there would be no
ultimate significance to the message of the saving Love of God,
expressed, for example in John 3:16: 'God so loved the world that
he gave his one and only Son, that whoever believes in him shall
not perish but have eternal life.'

The absolute togetherness and oneness in being and doing
between the crucified Jesus Christ and the Lord God is of supreme
importance for our belief in the Love of God. That was the truth
made clear by St Paul in his Epistle to the Romans, when he had in
mind the Old Testament account of the 'sacrifice' of Isaac by
Abraham, when Abraham showed that he loved God more than
he loved himself. And so St Paul wrote: 'If God is for us, who can
be against us? He who did not spare his own Son, but gave him up
for us all - how will he not also, along with him, graciously give us
all things?' (Rom 8:31-32). Jesus is God's very own Son, his only
begotten Son - one who came to us out of the Father's Life who
belonged to his very Heart and innermost Self. And when the Father
did not spare his own Son but freely delivered him up for us all in
atoning sacrifice, the Cross became a window into the innermost
heart of God and the nature of his Love. It tells us that God loves
us more than he loves himself.

That is what the oneness in being and act between Jesus Christ
and God, between the incarnate Son and the Father, reveals to us:
that our heavenly Father loves us more than he loves himself - and
we are assured of an infinite love from which nothing in life or
death can ever separate us. The love of the Lord Jesus in giving
himself for us on the Cross for our salvation, where the infinite
sacrifice of the Father and the infinite sacrifice of the Son are for
ever bound up indivisibly together, assures us that the eternal God,
let it be repeated, loves us more than he loves himself. God loves us
with an infinite love from which nothing in life or death can ever
separate us. That is the love incarnate in the Lord Jesus.

The Oneness of the Father and the Son:
In The Last Things

And what are we to think of the relation of Jesus Christ to 'the last things', the ultimate judgement of God and the consummation of his Kingdom? The Gospel assures us that even there Jesus Christ and God are not to be divided and that we will never be separated from his saving love incarnate in Christ, whatever may happen to us in this world. The eternal togetherness and oneness in being and act between Christ and God affirms for us belief in the one Lord Jesus Christ who will come again with glory to judge the quick and the dead, and whose Kingdom shall have no end. That is to say, the oneness of being between Jesus Christ and God that characterised the incarnation is not something of merely temporary duration in the economy of salvation: it is a final reality enduring endlessly into eternity.

Therefore, even on the 'last day' when God will judge the world, it will take place by the man Jesus Christ, who suffered and was buried and rose again and ascended to heaven and is enthroned at the right hand of God. Jesus is identified with the ultimate executive authority and power of God himself. Once again, everything hinges on the oneness of being between the incarnate Son and God the Father. That oneness is the ontic foundation that withstood the fearful strain and ordeal of the crucifixion and came through unbroken in the resurrection of Jesus Christ. As such, it correlates Jesus Christ ontologically and indivisibly with God Almighty in our final destiny as human beings.

That is something which, according to the witness of the New Testament, people were already aware of in the immediate presence of Jesus, for face to face with him they knew themselves to be face to face with the immediate presence and ultimate judgements of God. Even in the word of forgiveness which Jesus spoke to them they knew that he was forgiving them with the authority and prerogative of God himself the Judge of all the earth. The voice of divine forgiveness and the voice of divine judgement are one and the same. This unity belongs to the very heart of salvation mediated through Jesus. Such was the salvation they found actualised for them in the passion and resurrection of Jesus. As the Fourth Gospel expressed it, 'the Father judges no one, but has entrusted all judgement to the Son' (John 5:22). In our death as in our life God acts toward us only in and through his beloved Son. The judgements of God operate in and through his holiness and love incarnate in the Lord Jesus, and are mediated in and through him alone. While they are acts of the holiness and love of God, they are none other than the acts the Lord Jesus Christ such as we read of in the Gospels. God does not and will not act toward any one in life or death in any other way than he has done, does do, and will do in Jesus.

What would become of this Gospel if there were no oneness of being, or therefore of agency, between Jesus Christ and the Father, if there were at the end no ultimate blending of the forgiving love of Jesus and the final judgements of God? What would it mean for humankind if in the last resort in spite of all the Gospels tell us about Jesus, in spite of his self-sacrifice on the Cross, there is no real bridge in being or nature between him and God? It would surely mean that in the final analysis Jesus Christ, with all he stands for, is irrelevant for the ultimate destiny of men and women, and that the really decisive issues belong to God alone, and to a God whose love fell short of identifying himself with us in Jesus Christ to the extent of actually becoming one with us in and through him.

Any such detachment or disjunction between the being and nature of Jesus and the being and nature of God could only disrupt the message of grace and peace which the Gospel brings, and it would introduce the deepest anxiety into human life born of the dreadful fear that God may turn out in the end to be utterly different from what we see in Jesus Christ, fear lest there is behind the back of Jesus some dark inscrutable God, some arbitrary Deity of whom we can know nothing but before whom in our guilty conscience as sinners we cannot but quake and shiver in our souls. There is no doubt about the fact that this is a very real fear, as every genuine pastor of souls knows well. And it is a fear that results from a seriously damaged belief in the Deity of Christ whenever the bond of being between Christ and the Father is severed in their understanding of him. It is a fear that becomes an insistent nameless dread when the wounded conscience of the sinner, in its failure to receive a word of forgiveness and peace that is completely substantiated by the ultimate Being and Reality of God, can only turn in upon itself in a pathological twisting of the truth, so that the sinner paints harsh angry streaks upon the face of God as he imagines him behind the back of Jesus.

There is No God Behind the Back of Jesus

Already in the New Testament the Jesus of the Fourth Gospel was concerned to counter just such a distortion of people's understanding of God arising out of a damaged knowledge of him, and a divorce between belief in himself and belief in God the Father. He insisted that he and the Father were one (John 10:30), that what his Father had been doing hitherto he was continuing to do in an unbroken continuity of divine activity, he who had seen Jesus had seen the Father, so that there was no ground for anxiety or fear. What the Father is and does, Jesus is and does. And what Jesus is and does, the Father is and does. There is in fact no God behind the back of Jesus, no act of God other than the act of Jesus, no God but the God we see and meet in him. Jesus Christ is the open heart of God, the very love and life of God poured out to redeem humankind, the mighty hand and power of God stretched out to heal and save sinners. All things are in God's hands, but the hands of God and the hands of Jesus, in life and in death, are the same. That is to say, the ultimate destiny of humanity is bound up with Jesus Christ, for it is he who has come to invade and destroy the barrier of death and all that separates men and women from God. And it will be his voice, the voice of one through whom all divine judgement is channelled, the voice of Jesus, that will reach into the grave, and summon the dead into resurrection and life. For Jesus is himself the resurrection and the life with ultimate control over the destiny and future of each of those who believe in him.

That is the sense of the Holy Scripture to which the Early Church in the Nicene Creed gave precision, in its expression of the unqualified correlation in being and act between the Father and the Son. It declared that 'the one Lord Jesus Christ, the only begotten Son of God, begotten of his Father before all worlds, God of God, Light of Light, very God of very God, begotten not made, being of one substance with the Father, by whom all things were made shall come again with glory to judge both the quick and the dead, whose Kingdom shall have no end'. In other words, God is inherently and antecedently in himself, and will be to all eternity, what he has revealed himself to be in Jesus Christ.

Therefore, God is not one thing in Christ and another thing in himself. He has not shown us one face in Jesus Christ but kept his real face hidden from us behind the inscrutability of his ultimate unknowableness. He has not sent Jesus Christ to be a mere messenger whose words and deeds of love he does not back up with the pledge of his own Being and Reality and Love. On the contrary, God has wholly and unconditionally committed himself to us in the Incarnation of his dear Son in Jesus Christ, so that all that he eternally is and will be as God Almighty is pledged in Jesus Christ for us and our salvation. Jesus Christ and God are so utterly one in being and action that God does not, cannot, go back on Jesus Christ and his Cross. For that is who God is, he who came in Jesus Christ, and that is what God does, what Jesus Christ does.

Here we must remember the Ascension of the Lord Jesus and its saving significance. Complementing the Incarnation in which the eternal God himself condescended to be one with us in our hurt and creaturely disintegration in order to redeem us from all evil and to recreate us from within the ontological depths of our existence, and complementing the Passion and Resurrection of Jesus in which he accomplished this saving mission, is the Ascension of Jesus to the right hand of God the Father. There he who is bone of our bone and flesh of our flesh ever lives as our High Priest who through the consummation of his self-sacrifice as the Lamb of God makes intercession for us. As such he is enthroned at the summit of all being as the reconciling centre of all things visible and invisible. He is none other than our Lord Jesus, the incarnation of the Love of God, in whom and around whom all things revolve in the relation of God to humanity and humanity to God, whose Kingdom, as the Nicene Creed affirms, will have no end.

The Oneness Between the Father, the Son: the Holy Spirit

In the writings of the New Testament reference is often made to the Father and the Son, without explicit mention of the Holy Spirit who like the Son is one in being with the Father. That does not detract from the Deity of the Spirit, but is in line with what Jesus himself said when he taught the disciples about the Person and work of the Spirit whom the Father would send them in his name to lead them into the truth. He would not speak of himself, but would take of the things of Christ and deepen their understanding of them (John 16:13-16). That is to say, the Holy Spirit effaces himself or hides himself, as it were, behind Christ, and far from drawing attention to himself focuses the attention of people upon Christ and glorifies him.

The mission of the Spirit sent from the Father in the name of the Son as the Spirit of truth is to convict people of the truth as it is in Jesus, in judgement and mercy, to enlighten, inform and strengthen the Church through serving the centrality of Christ and deepening its understanding of his teaching and person as the incarnate Son of the Father, the one Lord and Saviour of humanity. The Holy Spirit is no less divine than the Father and the Son, but is the holy presence of God in and through whose communion we may know the grace of the Lord Jesus Christ and the love of God the Father. It is in and through him that the love of God is poured out into the hearts of men and women, confirming them in their faith. And by the Spirit, the Church of the Lord Jesus is endowed with power from on high for its ministry of the Gospel.

As the early Church realised, the key truth upon which the Church's proclamation of the Gospel and understanding of the Christian Faith rested is the oneness in being and act between the incarnate Son and God the Father. It was understanding and experience of that oneness that was reinforced and deepened by the indwelling illumination of the Holy Spirit. However, if that relation between Christ and the Father were severed or were held to be a merely an external or moral relation, as some heretics claimed, or (which amounts to the same thing) if the relation between the divine and human natures in the one Person of Christ were held to be only a moral union between two persons, a divine and a human, as other heretics would have it, then the Christological and Trinitarian structure of the Christian faith would be thrown into internal contradiction and confusion.

It was that threat to the very substance and integrity of the Gospel centred in the Lordship of Jesus Christ as the incarnate Son of God that prompted the vigour and passion with which the theological debates were pursued in early centuries first about the Deity of Christ and then about the Deity of the Holy Spirit. The great theologians of the fourth, fifth and sixth centuries saw clearly that the Christian Gospel could not take permanent root in that ancient culture so long as the dualist modes of thought embedded in it kept on undermining Christian understanding of the personal indivisible unity between Jesus Christ and God, and consequently between the Holy Spirit and God. Hence in the course of those centuries they confronted the dualist thought of the Graeco-Roman culture with the non-dualist Judaeo-Christian outlook upon the created universe, and sought to transform the very foundations of ancient philosophy and science as well as religion. It was only as Nicene theology went together with that kind of transformation that the Christian Church, with its evangelical and its theological understanding and way of life, became established in the Mediterranean world, grounded in the centrality of the Lord Jesus Christ as true God of true God.

To conclude, it is through the oneness of being between Jesus Christ and God the Father together with the oneness of being between the Holy Spirit and both the Father and the Son, that we are led to express the truth that what God is toward us in the condescension of his love and self-revelation in Jesus Christ as Father, Son and Holy Spirit, he is antecedently and eternally in the Communion of in his own eternal Being. That is to say, the specific forms of God's self-revelation and incarnate self-communication to us through the Grace of the Lord Jesus Christ, the Love of God and the Communion of the Holy Spirit, are not just transient forms of his self-revelation to us in space and time, but are eternally inherent in him as One God Three Persons.

Stoking the Fire

1 In what events from the life of Jesus do we see the oneness between the Father and the Son?

2 What do we gain by embracing the reality that 'what Jesus is and does, the Father is and does'?

3 But what, according to Thomas Torrance, happens to us if we imagine that there is a God behind the back of Jesus Christ?

4 On what basis can Torrance make the claim that in Jesus we see that 'God loves us more than he loves himself'? How do you respond to that statement?

5 What is the role of the Holy Spirit in revealing who Jesus is, and why may it be described as humble?

6 Where in the church today do you see the oneness between the Son and the Father denied or neglected? What can the church do to recover this essential, wonderful truth?

Ignition Points

He made our lost and damned condition, our death under divine judgement, his very own.

'The faith of the Son of God' is to be understood here not just as my faith in him, but as the faith of Christ himself, for it refers primarily to Christ's unswerving faithfulness, his vicarious and substitutionary faith which embraces and undergirds us, such that when we believe we must say with St Paul 'not I but Christ', even in our act of faith.

It is in Christ's grasp of us rather than in our grasp of him that our salvation and certainty lie.

It is thus that our grasp of faith, feeble though it is, is grasped and enfolded in the mighty grasp of Christ who identifies himself with us, and puts himself in our place, making what is ours wholly his own, so that we may have wholly made over to us what is Christ's.

In far too much preaching of Christ the ultimate responsibility is taken off the shoulders of the Lamb of God and put upon the shoulders of the poor sinners, and we know well in our hearts that we cannot cope with it.

That is to say, if people are damned, they are damned by the Gospel.

Without any doubt the Gospel of unconditional grace is very difficult for us, for it is so costly. It takes away from under our feet the very ground on which we want to stand, and the free-will which we as human beings cherish so dearly becomes exposed as a subtle form of self-will - no one is free to escape from his self-will. It is the costliness of unconditional grace that people resent.

Chapter Two
PREACHING JESUS CHRIST
Thomas F. Torrance

As we prepare to preach the gospel, Thomas Torrance
reminds us of 'the unconditional nature of salvation
by grace.' Our focus is ever on Jesus Christ, who
gave himself completely and freely for us. We must
never unwittingly cast people back on themselves.
For the gospel is always 'Not I, but Christ'. The first
concern of preaching, then, is 'in Christ's grasp of us
rather than in our grasp of him'. In Christ Jesus alone
does 'our salvation and certainty lie'. And this word
is the wisdom of God to enlighten our age.

'For I resolved to know nothing while I was with you except Jesus
Christ and him crucified. I came to you in weakness and fear, and
with much trembling. My message and my preaching were not
with wise and persuasive words, but with a demonstration of the
Spirit's power, so that your faith might not rest on men's wisdom,
but on God's power' (1 Cor 2:2-5).

The Cross of Christ surely lies at the heart of our faith and of
the mission of the Gospel. 'God crucified', as Gregory Nazianzen
expressed it, is the most astonishing part of the Christian gospel.
This identification of the Man on the Cross with God himself is, as
St Paul once wrote, offence to the Jews and foolishness to the
Greeks. Be that as it may, it is the preaching of Christ crucified
that lies at the very centre of the Christian Gospel. The Cross, as
H.R. Mackintosh once wrote in a Gospel tract, is 'a window into
the heart of God'. He was drawing attention there to the words of
St Paul, 'He who did not spare his own Son, but gave him up for us
all - how will he not also, along with him, graciously give us all
things?' (Rom 8:31-32). We saw in the last chapter how, in giving
his own dear Son to die for us in atoning sacrifice for the sins of the

world, God has revealed that he loves us more than he loves himself. So, far from remaining detached from us in our fearful alienation and unappeasable agony, God has penetrated through the Cross into the deepest depths of our wickedness and violence and taken it all upon himself in order to judge it and redeem us from their tyranny over us.

If the Church is to be faithful to its calling it must concentrate on the uniqueness of Christ, and particularly on Christ clothed with his Gospel as the crucified and risen Lord. It is through the Gospel of the saving love of God exhibited and enacted in the atoning sacrifice of Christ that the life and faith of the Church are found to be rooted and grounded in the incarnate act of the Son of God in becoming one with us as we really are. He made our lost and damned condition, our death under divine judgement, his very own. I believe we have to stress again and again the fact that in the Incarnation and the Cross, Christ has penetrated into the darkest depths of our abject human misery and perdition where he takes our place, intercedes for us, substitutes himself for us, and makes the atoning restitution which we could not make, thereby reconciling us to God in the Holy Spirit as his dear children.

Now in preaching this, I believe that it is concentration upon the vicarious humanity of Christ in the Incarnation and Atonement, in death and resurrection, that is particularly important for us today. It is curious that evangelicals often link the substitutionary act of Christ only with his death, and not with his incarnate Person and life - that is dynamite for them! They thereby undermine the radical nature of substitution, what the New Testament calls *katallage*, or Christ in our place and Christ for us in every respect. Substitution understood in this radical way means that Christ takes our place in all our human life and activity before God, even in our believing, praying and worshipping of God, for he has yoked himself to us in such a profound way that he stands in for us, and upholds us at every point in our human relations before God.

Preaching the Faith of the Son of God

Galatians 2:20 has long been for me a passage of primary importance as it was for my fathers in the faith, John McLeod Campbell and Hugh R. Mackintosh: 'I am crucified with Christ, nevertheless I live, yet not I. But Christ lives in me, and the life which I now live in the flesh, I live by the faith of the Son of God,

who loved me and gave himself for me' (author's translation). 'The
faith of the Son of God' is to be understood here not just as my
faith in him, but as the faith of Christ himself, for it refers primarily
to Christ's unswerving faithfulness, his vicarious and substitutionary
faith which embraces and undergirds us, such that when we believe
we must say with Paul 'not I but Christ', even in our act of faith.
This is not in any way to denigrate the human act of faith on our
part, for it is only in and through the vicarious faith of Christ that
we can truly and properly believe. Faith in Christ involves a polar
relation between the faith of Christ and our faith, in which our faith
is laid hold of, enveloped and upheld by his unswerving faithfulness.
No human being can do that for another, far less give himself as a
ransom from his sin, but this is precisely what the Lord Jesus does
when in giving himself for us he completely takes our place, makes
our cause his very own in every respect, and yields to the heavenly
Father the response of faith and love which we are altogether
incapable of yielding.

It is the same conception of faith, I believe, that is found in St
Paul's teaching that we are justified by faith and that the just shall
live by faith. Does this mean that the just person lives from his
own faith or from God's faith? In saying that 'The righteous will
live by faith' (Rom 1:17), the apostle was actually citing from the
book of Habakkuk (2:4), but in the Habakkuk Commentary found
among the Dead Sea Scrolls this is interpreted to mean that the just
live from 'the faith of God', which is also, incidentally, the way
that people like Athanasius, Calvin, and Barth have interpreted it.
However, if we understand faith in the polar way to which I have
pointed, justice can be done to both conceptions of faith! In the
polar relation the primary pole is certainly God's faith or Christ's
faith, for he is the faithful one who lays hold of us and brings us
into a living relation with himself, but within the embrace of that
relation the secondary pole is that of the believer, his responding
faith. But that is an act of faith that is evoked by and sustained by
the faithfulness of God - far from being of ourselves, it is a gift of
God. This is how, I am sure, we are to understand the relation of
our response in faith to the vicarious faith of Christ. The Pauline
principle 'Not I but Christ' applies to faith: 'I believe, yet not I but
Christ'.

The Reconciling Exchange

When preaching about faith in Christ and his vicarious humanity I sometimes use and develop an illustration taken from John Welsh, the son-in-law of John Knox, who used to point out that our grasping of Christ by faith is itself enclosed within the mighty grasp of Christ, and it is in Christ's grasp of us rather than in our grasp of him that our salvation and certainty lie. In this connection I sometimes recall what happened when my daughter was learning to walk. I took her by the hand to help her, and I can still feel her little fingers tightly clutching my hand. She was not relying on her feeble grasp of my hand, but on my strong grasp of her hand, and even my grasping of her grasping of my hand.

Is that not how we are to understand the faith by which we lay hold of Christ as our Saviour? It is thus that our grasp of faith, feeble though it is, is grasped and enfolded in the mighty grasp of Christ who identifies himself with us, and puts himself in our place, making what is ours wholly his own, so that we may have wholly made over to us what is Christ's. Think of that in terms of St Paul's wonderful statement, 'For you know the grace of our Lord Jesus Christ, that though he was rich, yet for your sakes he became poor, so that you through his poverty might become rich' (2 Cor 8:9) That is what the early Church and John Calvin called the 'the blessed exchange' or 'the wondrous exchange', and even the Roman Missal calls *mirabile commercium* (wonderful trade). This is in fact the New Testament doctrine of *katallage* (substitution), for it is an atoning and reconciling exchange, in which what is ours is displaced by Christ who substituted himself in our place and yet is restored in a new way to us.

A very important point must be noted here, relating to the fact that in his becoming one of us and one with us as we actually are, Christ takes our sins upon himself in such a way as to make them serve our healing and salvation. Think of the incident in the Gospel when James and John quite selfishly asked for the privilege of being at the right hand and left hand of Jesus at the inauguration of his Kingdom, which made the other disciples angry. Jesus did not rebuke them, except to ask if they could drink of the cup that he drank of and be baptised with the baptism with which he was baptised. When they said they could, he promised that they would indeed drink of the cup that he drank of and be baptised with the baptism with which he was baptised (Mark 10:35-40).

A little later, Jesus sat down with his disciples at the Passover Meal at which he specifically linked his body and blood with the Covenant. Then when Jesus was betrayed and crucified the disciples found themselves in utter disarray standing before the Cross in a crowd of people who mocked and jeered at Jesus and laughed at the helplessness of Jesus nailed to the Cross. Jesus was now utterly alone, abandoned by them, and they the disciples were now separated from him by an unbridgeable chasm of shame and betrayal and horror, for they had all forsaken him and fled. They had betrayed the very love with which he had bound them to himself. Then they remembered what had happened at the Upper Room and the Covenant Jesus had forged with them in his body and blood. Jesus had meant them to remember, for in that act he took their very sins, even their denial of him, and used it as the very means by which to bind them to himself.

Then the disciples understood the significance of the vicarious Passion of Christ as something undertaken not for the righteous, but precisely for the sinner. It was their very sin, their betrayal, their shame, their unworthiness, which became in the inexplicable love of God the very material he laid hold of, and turned into the bond that bound them to the crucified Messiah, to the salvation and love of God forever. That is the way in which the *katallage*, the wondrous exchange of the atoning and reconciling Cross of Christ operates, by making the shameful things that divide us from him, into the very things that bind us to him in life and death for ever. Such is the unlimited power of the Cross of Christ.

Preaching The Gospel at the Lord's Supper

It is not easy to preach the truth that we are saved by the Grace of Christ alone, and that it is through the vicarious humanity of Jesus and in its substitutionary bearing upon faith that we can properly believe, but this is what may be proclaimed at Holy Communion as nowhere else. In my Scottish tradition the great revivals have often taken place in connection with the celebration of the Lord's Supper, for example the great revival in the middle of the eighteenth century at Shotts Kirk (where incidentally, my grandparents are buried).

I have found in my own ministry that it is easiest to preach the unconditional nature of grace, and the vicarious humanity and substitutionary role of Christ in faith, at the celebration of the

Eucharist, where the call for repentance and faith is followed by
Communion in the Body and Blood of Christ in which we stretch
out empty hands to receive the bread and wine: 'Nothing in my
hands I bring, simply to the Cross I cling'.

There at the Holy Table I know that I cannot rely on my own
faith but only on the vicarious faith of the Lord Jesus in the total
substitution of his atoning sacrifice on the Cross. Salvation and
justification are by the grace of God alone. Faith, as John Calvin
taught, is an empty vessel, so that when you approach the Table of
the Lord, it is not upon your faith that you rely, but upon Christ
and his Cross alone. That is what the Covenant in his body and
blood which the Saviour has forged for us actually, practically and
really means. It is of the very essence of the Gospel that salvation
and justification are by the grace of Christ alone, in which he takes
your place, that you may have his place.

I believe this emphasis in the mission of the Church may well
be more important than anything else today. There is a kind of
subtle Pelagianism* in preaching and teaching which has the effect
of throwing people back in the last resort on their own act of faith,
so that in the last analysis responsibility for their salvation rests
upon themselves, rather than Christ. In far too much preaching of
Christ the ultimate responsibility is taken off the shoulders of the
Lamb of God and put upon the shoulders of the poor sinners, and
we know well in our hearts that we cannot cope with it. Is that not
one of the things that keeps pushing people away from the Kirk? I
think here of the reluctance of many people to approach the Holy
Table, which happens on Communion Sundays when people fail
to understand the absolutely free and unconditional nature of the
Grace of the Lord Jesus Christ. He came not to call the righteous
but sinners to repentance. Through the miracle of his Cross, he
turns our sins and failings into the very means he uses in order to
save us and bind us to himself. That is precisely what he pledges to
us in the Communion of his Body and Blood.

---

* The doctrine taught by Pelagius, the great opponent of Augustine, that we
can become righteous through the exercise of our free wills (ed.)

Unconditional Grace

Let us pause for a minute to reflect on the nature and implications of unconditional grace as it is freely extended to us in forgiveness. One does not forgive an innocent person but only a guilty one - by its very nature forgiveness involves a judgement on the wrongdoer. Total forgiveness involves total judgement, and it is total forgiveness that Christ gives us which involves a total judgement upon us. Think of that in terms of the Cross, on which Christ died for us, all of us, and the whole of each one of us, not just a part of us. Hence we must think that the whole of our being comes under the judgement of the Cross. That is why, as H.R. Mackintosh used to say, at the Lord's Supper as we partake of the body and blood of Christ, we feel ashamed of our whole being, for our goodness as well as our badness. In the atoning exchange of Grace in which Christ gave himself for us, all that we are and claim to be, is called in question.

There is no such thing as a partial substitution, or therefore a partial forgiveness and a partial judgement. Each one of us comes unreservedly under the judgement of the Cross, for in his act of total self-substitution Christ took the place of each one of us in making our sin his own and in bearing it along with the judgement of God upon it. Christ Jesus died for us when we were yet sinners; hence we must think him as having died for all people while they are yet sinners irrespective of their response. Just as the Cross is proclaimed to all, so the total forgiveness and the total judgement it involves are proclaimed to all, whether they believe or not. But unconditional forgiveness involves unconditional judgement. Just as divine forgiveness is not given on the ground of some condition being met by us, so the judgement it involves, the judgement enacted and exhibited on the Cross once for all, is likewise unconditioned.

This unconditional grace of the Lord Jesus Christ which is proclaimed to us in the Gospel summons us to repent and believe. But in our very act of believing and repenting, we with our faith, with our believing and repenting self, come under the unconditional judgement of Christ's forgiveness. Face to face with the Lord Jesus whose eyes search out the deepest secrets of our being and whose Spirit discerns the thoughts and intents of the heart, all our acts of faith and repentance, our prayer and worship, are found to be unclean in God's sight, so that if divine forgiveness were conditional on our responses, we would never be saved. Even the exercise of our free-will in believing and repenting in response to the summons of the Gospel is not separable from our self-will, for it is the self in our free-will and self-will, the subtle Pelagianism of the human heart, that comes under the judgement of Christ's unconditional forgiveness. We sinful human beings are trapped by our sin within the circle of our hearts which are turned in upon themselves, so that we cannot even repent of our faith or repent of our repentance, but are cast wholly and unreservedly upon the unconditional forgiveness of Christ Jesus. Indeed it is because the judgement inherent in his forgiveness falls upon the innermost self in all our acts of faith and repentance, that we are thrown upon Christ alone and are saved by grace alone.

Without any doubt the Gospel of unconditional grace is very difficult for us, for it is so costly. It takes away from under our feet the very ground on which we want to stand, and the free-will which we as human beings cherish so dearly becomes exposed as a subtle form of self-will - no one is free to escape from his self-will. It is the costliness of unconditional grace that people resent. Martin Luther once said that when he preached justification by faith alone, people responded to it like a cow staring at a new gate, but he also said that when he preached justification by grace alone it provoked tumults. I find this kind of disturbance again and again in the reaction not only of people outside the Church, but even of would-be evangelical people within the membership of Church, for their refusal to accept unconditional grace seems to be due to the fact that it cuts so deeply into the quick of their souls.

This is part of what I meant a short time ago when I pointed out that there is a subtle form of Pelagianism in the way people often preach the Gospel and claim that people will be saved only if they believe, or on condition that they believe. Hidden deep down beneath all that there is a failure to take the New Testament teaching about the power of the Cross of Christ and his substitutionary role seriously, a reluctance to allow it to apply to the whole of their being and to all their human activity before God, even to their believing and praying and worshipping. We need to learn and learn again and again that salvation by grace alone is so radical that we have to rely upon Christ Jesus entirely in everything, and that it is only when we rely on him alone that we are really free to believe: 'Not I but Christ' yet 'Christ in me'. Because he came as man to take our place, in and through his humanity our humanity is radically transformed, and we become truly human and really free to believe, love and serve him. That is the wonderful message of the Cross and Resurrection.

What of Those That Turn Away?

I have been laying the emphasis upon the unconditional nature of salvation by grace grounded in the fact that Christ gave himself freely in atoning sacrifice for all people without exception, for that is what we are sent by our Lord to preach. But what of those who turn away from the Gospel and its summons to repent and believe? They do not thereby nullify the unconditional nature of the grace of Christ, or therefore the unconditional nature of the divine judgement which it involves. The judgement of God upon sinners remains when they spurn his grace. While the preaching of the Gospel, in the vivid expression of St Paul, is to some people a vital fragrance that brings life, to others it is a deadly fume that kills (2 Cor 2:16). That is to say, if people are damned, they are damned by the Gospel. Why anyone who is freely offered the unconditional grace and love of God in the Lord Jesus should turn away from him, is something quite inexplicable and baffling to those who are 'on the way to salvation', but it is a fearful fact that the New Testament will not allow preachers of the Gospel to ignore or forget its teaching about damnation. It is at the final judgement that the dark side of the Cross, the unconditional judgement of God upon all sin and evil, will be unveiled, for people will be judged by what took place once for all in the finished work of Christ on the Cross, when he was crucified as the Lamb of God to bear and bear away the sins of the world. Is that not what the New Testament speaks of as 'the wrath of the Lamb'? Jesus said, 'Whoever believes and is baptised will be saved, but whoever does not believe will be condemned' (Mark 16:16).

It was one of the lovely and refreshing things about the preaching of Billy Graham during his last tour of Scotland that in preaching Christ, he directed people to Christ and to Christ alone as Lord and Saviour. Through such a direct and blunt way, even more than through brilliant preaching, the Holy Spirit challenged thousands and thousands of people who were not members of the Church, and thousands who were under thirty years of age with the Gospel. They turned in their utter helplessness to Christ Jesus, to find in him one who has wholly taken their place so that they might freely be given his place. It is in this message of the unconditional grace and vicarious humanity of the Lord Jesus Christ that people have often told me that they have found healing and liberation which they never thought possible.

The Wisdom and Power of God

Let me now end by directing attention back to those two passages in St Paul's First Epistle to the Corinthians (1:17-18 & 2:2-5) and through them to the Cross of Christ as the power of God, and to the kind of faith that does not stand in human wisdom, but in the power of God.

I believe that emphatic focus upon this truth is precisely what is very much needed in the Church today in its calling to preach Christ. This is the central truth that we must surely stress in the ministry of ministers, elders and deacons, and church workers alike, and in the Christian witness of every member of the Church. It is the one message that really reaches the multitudes that are outside the Church, the young as well as the old. Unfortunately the kind of evangelism that is so often most vociferous actually seems to blur the radical nature of Christ's vicarious humanity and the New Testament Gospel that proclaims it. That kind of 'evangelism' itself needs to be evangelised! The Gospel must be proclaimed in an evangelical way! It is the proclamation of the Cross as the power of God, and teaching about faith standing in the power of God not in human wisdom, foolish as it may look before the wisdom of the world, that will open wide the gates and point the way ahead for a radical renewal of the Church and its mission. That is the kind of wisdom, the wisdom of God, as St Paul called it, that we in the Churches desperately need today.

In the celebration of the Eucharist in the Orthodox Church, it is when the Holy Gospel is lifted up and carried forth that there rings out through the Church a loud shout from the priest standing in front of the congregation, 'Here is Wisdom'. Yes, it is in the celebration of the Lord's Supper that proclamation of the Lord's death and the Wisdom of God come so effectively together in the life and ministry of the Church, for it is at the Eucharist where we rely wholly upon Christ, and his Cross, not at all upon ourselves, that true wisdom is to be found, the Wisdom of God!

Stoking the Fire

1 What does Thomas Torrance mean by the phrase, 'the vicarious humanity' of Christ?

2 What are the implications of the idea that Christ's substitution for us was not only on the Cross for our sins but in his whole life as a human being on our behalf?

3 In the 'reconciling exchange', mentioned on p.26, what is shipped out from us to Christ and what is shipped in from Christ to us?

4 Under these grace-filled arrangements, what use does Christ make of 'the shameful things that divide us from him'?

5 What is the dark, costly side to us in the unconditional grace and total forgiveness of Christ?

6 How do you interpret the statement, 'If people are damned, they are damned by the Gospel'?

7 Explain how the dynamic of 'Not I but Christ, yet Christ in me' might work in your life.

Ignition Points

God does not accept us because we have offered worthy worship. In his love, he accepts us freely in the Person of his beloved Son, who in our name and on our behalf, in our humanity, has made the one offering to the Father, which alone is acceptable to God for all humanity.

If the first way can engender weariness, this second way - the way of grace - releases joy and ecstasy, for with inward peace we are lifted up out of ourselves by the Spirit into a world of praise and adoration and communion in Christ.

Christ does not heal us by standing over against us, diagnosing our sickness, prescribing medicine for us to take, and then going away, to leave us to get better by obeying his instructions - as an ordinary doctor might. No, He becomes the patient! He assumes that very humanity which is in need of redemption, and by being anointed by the Spirit in our humanity, by a life of perfect obedience, by dying and rising again, for us, our humanity is healed in him!

Christ deals with humanity on the part of God and deals with God on behalf of humanity.

We are certainly summoned unconditionally to a life of faith and repentance, but our response of evangelical repentance is now by the grace of God, through the Spirit, a response to a Response - our response to the Word of the Cross - made in virtue of our union with Christ.

Chapter 3
CHRIST IN OUR PLACE
James B. Torrance

James Torrance examines what the doctrine of the vicarious humanity of Christ in our place means for our worship. He distinguishes between our usual view of worship as something that we do and the reality that true Christian worship is a participation in what Christ has done and is doing. We partake of his communion with the Father. Jesus fulfils both the God-humanward movement of worship and the human-Godward response demanded of us in worship. So we see that all our worship takes place in Christ. We participate in his communion with the Father, and so we are lifted beyond ourselves, not by our own merit, into the grace of the Triune God.

What is the right way to worship God? The biblical answer to this question is simply, 'through Jesus Christ'. The meaning of that in turn is expressed by the Nicene Creed.

The Nicene Creed emerged out of the worship of the Church, and is therefore concerned about the place of Jesus Christ in worship. The historical statements made about Jesus in the New Testament and the preaching of the early Church gave rise to both doxological and theological statements such as we find in the ancient Creeds - to adoration, praise, prayer, to the confession 'Thou art the King of glory, O Christ, thou art the everlasting Son of the Father'. The Nicene Creed is a powerful doxological thatement about the Person of Christ: Jesus Christ is 'very God of very God, begotten, not made, of one substance with the Father... Who for us men and our salvation came down from heaven... And was crucified also for us under Pontius Pilate.'

Worship above all requires an understanding of 'Christ in our place'.

Two Different views of Worship

As I see it, there are broadly two different views of worship in the Church today.

1 The first view, probably the commonest and most widespread, is that worship is something which we do - mainly in Church on Sunday. We go to Church, we sing our psalms to God, we intercede for Northern Ireland or the Middle East, we listen to the sermon (too often simply an exhortation), we offer our money, time and talents to God. No doubt we need God's grace to help us do it; we do it because Jesus taught us to do it and left us an example to show us how to do it. But worship is what WE do.

In theological language, this means that the only priesthood is our priesthood, the only offering our offering, the only intercessions our intercessions.

This view of worship is in practice unitarian. It has no doctrine of the Mediator or the Sole Priesthood of Christ. It is human-centred, with no proper doctrine of the Holy Spirit, and is basically non-sacramental. It engenders weariness. We sit in the pew watching the minister 'doing his/her thing', exhorting us 'to do our thing', until we go home thinking we have done our duty for another week! This kind of 'do-it-yourself-with-the-help-of-the-minister' worship is what our forebears would have called 'legal' worship, and not 'evangelical' worship. It is what the ancient church would have called 'Arian' or 'Pelagian', and not truly catholic.

2 The second view is that worship is rather the gift of participating through the Spirit in the incarnate Son's communion with the Father - of participating, in union with Christ, in what he has done for us once and for all in his life and death on the Cross, and in what he is continuing to do for us in the presence of the Father, and in his mission to the world. The bread which we break, is it not our sharing in the Body of Christ? The cup of blessing which we bless, is it not our sharing in the Blood of Christ? Our sonship and communion with the Father, are they not our sharing by the Spirit of adoption in his Sonship, are they not our sharing by the Spirit of adoption in his Sonship and communion with the Father? Our intercession for Northern Ireland and the Middle East, are they not our participation in Christ's intercession for Northern Ireland and the Middle East? Our mission to the world and ministry to the needs of humanity, are they not the gift of participating in

Christ's mission to the world and his ministry to human needs? Is this not the meaning of life in the Spirit?

This second view is trinitarian and incarnational. It takes seriously New Testament teaching about the sole Priesthood and Headship of Christ, the once-and-for-all self-offering of Christ, life in union with Christ through the Spirit, with a vision of the Church as the Body of Christ. It is fundamentally 'sacramental' - but in a way which enshrines the Gospel of grace, that God in the gift of Christ and the gift of the Spirit, gives us what he demands - the worship of our hearts and lives. This is the heart of our theology of the eucharist.

It was the concern of the Reformers to recover this New Testament and early Christian view of worship in a world where the medieval Church had tended to substitute the priesthood, the sacrifice, the merits, the intercession of the Church - the vicarious humanity of the *ecclesia* (Mary and the saints) - for the vicarious humanity of the Christ, in a way which obscured the Gospel of grace, the Good News of what God has done for us in Christ. The reformers saw clearly the significance of the Pauline teaching about justification, that we are accepted by God, not because of our 'good works', but freely by God's grace received in faith. They also saw clearly what this meant for our understanding of worship, that God does not accept us because we have offered worthy worship. In his love, he accepts us freely in the Person of his beloved Son, who in our name and on our behalf, in our humanity, has made the one offering to the Father, which alone is acceptable to God for all humanity, for all nations, for all times, and who unites us with himself in the one Body, in his communion with the Father.

This second view is both catholic and evangelical. Whereas the first view can be divisive, in that every church and denomination 'does its own thing' and worships God in its own way, this second way is unifying in that it recognises that there is only one way to come to the Father, namely, through Christ in the communion of the Spirit, in the communion of saints, whatever outward form our worship may take. If the first way can engender weariness, this second way - the way of grace - releases joy and ecstasy, for with inward peace we are lifted up out of ourselves by the Spirit into a world of praise and adoration and communion in Christ. On this view the vicarious humanity of Christ and union with Christ are foundational twin doctrines.

3 It might be argued that the distinction between these two views is drawn too sharply. Is there not a middle position, which is in fact probably the point of view of most church members? It might be stated in this way. Yes, worship is what we do - but we worship God, Father, Son and Holy Spirit, we pray to Christ as God, we invoke the Holy Spirit, we respond to the preaching of the Word, we intercede for the world, we offer our money, time and service to God, we remember the death of Jesus in the Sacrament.

This view might be defended on the ground of the 'priesthood of all believers' and as being trinitarian, but it falls short of the New Testament understanding of participation through the Spirit in what Christ has done and in what Christ is doing for us in our humanity. It is human-centred. It is a do-it-yourself-in-response-to-Christ worship, and is to this extent a modification of the first view, though with more Christian content. Its weakness is that it falls short of an adequate understanding of the role of the vicarious humanity of Christ and of the Spirit in our worship of the Father - of why Christ became man for us and our salvation.

It is the concern of this chapter to consider the role of the incarnate Christ in worship, for it is supremely in the context of worship that we see the importance of the Nicene doctrine of the Incarnation. In the New Testament, two things are held together, God comes to us as man in Christ, and therefore we pray to Christ as God. But on the other hand, Jesus is presented to us as our Brother, a weak, suffering, tempted, struggling human being, praying for us and with us to the Father, and uniting us with himself in his communion with the Father, and his intercession for the world. This is part of what is meant by Jesus being our only Priest. When the role of Christ in our humanity, in his life of worship and communion with the Father, is emphasised in this New Testament fashion, then our worship is seen as the gift of participating through the Spirit in Christ's communion with the Father. The Christ to whom we pray himself lived a life of prayer, and draws us into his life of prayer, putting his word 'Father' into our lips, so that our life of prayer might become 'the life of God in the soul of man'. By sharing Jesus' life of communion with the Father in the Spirit, we are given to participate in the eternal Son's communion with the Father in the Spirit.

Three Theological Models today

Before developing this further, consider the background to all this in the way Christian thought about the Incarnation has diverged from orthodox and biblical understanding.

1 The Liberal Model

The first model is that of nineteenth-century Protestant liberalism, recently revived by Professor John Hick. According to this, the heart of religion is the soul's immediate relationship to God. It can be expressed thus: What God the Father was to old Israel, he was to Jesus, and what he was to Jesus, he was to Paul and is the same to us and all humans today. We with Jesus stand as humans before God, as brothers and sisters worshipping the one Father, but not any incarnate Son. Jesus is man but not God.

In the words of the German thinker Adolf Harnack: 'The Gospel, as Jesus proclaimed it, has to do with the Father only and not with the Son. The Christian religion means, 'God and the soul, the soul and its God'; nothing must come between the child and its heavenly Father - be it priest, Bible, law, doctrine, or Jesus Christ himself! To Harnack, the Incarnation was something alien to the simple Gospel of Jesus.

This view is clearly unitarian, individualistic, and operates with a divorce between 'person and principle'. The important thing, said Harnack, is the principle of vicarious love and self-sacrifice, not the Person of Jesus. Jesus is significant as the supreme example of this principle. But this reduces Christianity to hero worship. On this view of Jesus, there is a basic mental dualism or dichotomy between history and idea, fact and meaning, happening and experience. In the words of another nineteenth century thinker, the historical element was 'no more than the means of introducing the Christian idea into history'.

Clearly if you come to the New Testament, to theology, with this sharp disjunction between person and principle, between the death of Jesus and the principle of vicarious heroic self-sacrifice, between fact and meaning (the divorce between the empirical and the theoretical), it is impossible to do justice to the uniqueness of Jesus. The doctrine of the Incarnation of God in Christ - that Jesus is God's 'only Son' - must go. On these premises, to make an absolute of Jesus is to make a myth out of him. That is why modern Liberals speak about 'The Myth of God Incarnate'.

But it was against just such a dualistic approach, in its Hellenic form in Arianism, that the Church Fathers contended, in expounding their biblical understanding of the place of Jesus Christ in worship. So far from the doctrine of the Incarnation being the Hellenising of the simple Gospel, the accommodation of the Gospel to Greek culture, the doctrine emerges most powerfully precisely where the Greek Fathers of the Church were hammering out in the teeth of their own dualistic culture, their biblical faith that God became man in Jesus. What could be more un-Hellenic than the statement of the Creed that God 'was made man'!

The question posed by the first model is this. Can we determine in advance what we may (or may not) find in history - what we may or may not believe? It is surely unscientific to allow our method or presuppositions to control or determine what we may believe or experience. A genuine openness to reality surely requires that it is the object of our enquiry and our worship which must prescribe both our mode of knowing and our mode of worship. In other words, we must take the claims of the Gospel writers seriously as they are presented, and not assume that they are some kind of 'myth'.

2 The Existential Model

Here again faith means something contemporary and immediate. God gives himself to us in grace in the present moment of encounter, and we respond in faith, but this response in faith is only made possible because of the work of Christ on the Cross.

On this model, we are accepted by God as forgiven, as his children today, because of the death of Jesus nineteen hundred years ago. The vicarious work of Jesus (his work on our behalf) is the instrumental cause of our present faith and experience of salvation. We are saved through Christ. The event of the Cross gives rise to the event of faith. The event a long time ago comes to us today through the event of preaching, sharing of the Gospel. However, on this view, the key thing is our decision, our commitment to believe. This can be understood in more radical terms (as in the theology of Rudolf Bultmann), or in more evangelical terms (as in the early Karl Barth). But Barth quickly came to see that this emphasis on the present moment of encounter can make the Incarnation itself of no significance. The idea of Incarnation, rather than the event and the Person, would be enough.

This model in its different forms seeks to do justice to the Reformed expressions, by grace alone, and by faith alone. But although it stresses how God comes to meet us in Christ, the movement from us to God is still our movement, our faith, our response! This theology short-circuits the vicarious humanity of Christ and belittles union with Christ. While it seems to emphasise the vicarious work of Christ on the Cross to bring forgiveness and make our faith a real human possibility, it fails to see the place of the high Priesthood of Christ as the One who leads our worship, bears our sorrows on his heart and intercedes for us, presenting us to the Father in himself as God's dear children and uniting us with himself in his life in the Spirit.

To reduce worship to this two-dimensional thing (God and ourselves today) is to imply that God throws us back on ourselves to make our response, and to ignore the fact that God has already provided for us that Response which alone is acceptable to him - the Offering made for humankind in the life, obedience and passion of Jesus Christ. But is this not to lose the comfort and peace of the Gospel, as well as the secret of true Christian prayer as the gift of sharing in the intercessions of Christ, that we do not know how to pray as we ought, but the Spirit makes intercession for us? Whatever else our faith is, it is a response to a Response already made for us and continually being made for us in Christ.

This existential model makes religious experience its starting point and central concern, and interprets the work of Christ in terms of human need and experience, and then seeks to interpret Christ's Person in terms of his work. But with such an 'event theology', we become more interested in the blessings of the Gospel which accrue to us from the work of Christ than in Christ himself, so that we can subtly separate the blessings of Christ from Christ, and the work of Christ from his Person - and even regard 'Incarnation' as just one optional way among others of accounting for the experience of salvation.

It was against this approach that Bonhoeffer made the plea that we give priority to the Who-question over the What and the How - that we interpret Atonement in terms of the Incarnation and not the other way round. For in the Nicene Creed, it is after the statement as to Who Christ is that there comes the phrase, 'who for us men and our salvation came down from heaven... and was made man, and was crucified for us under Pontius Pilate'. The Acts of God are interpreted in the light of his Being.

3 The Nicene, Incarnational Model

Here we come to the heart of Christian worship - that worship is the gift of participating in the incarnate Son's communion with the Father, and in so worshipping we worship and glorify the Father, the Son and the Holy Spirit. In the New Testament, Christ is presented as living a life of union and communion with the Father in the Spirit, presenting himself in our humanity through the eternal Spirit to the Father on behalf of all, and drawing us by his Spirit to participate both in his life of worship and in his mission from the Father to the world. There is thus established for us a twofold relationship, between God and humanity in Christ, and at the same time a relationship between Christ and the Church, both of which are understood in terms of the Holy Spirit, who is the bond of love between the Father and the Son, and the bond of love between Christ and his people.

The Nicene Fathers used the phrase '*homousios* with the Father' in speaking of how Jesus is related to the Father; it is a relationship which is both internal to the Godhead and externally established between God and humanity in the Incarnation. Here our concern is to see that fundamental to this model and this understanding of worship are the twin doctrines of vicarious humanity and union with Christ.

In the language of 1 John 1:3, 'Our fellowship is with the Father and with his Son Jesus Christ'. The early Church expressed this by saying that he who was the eternal Son of God by nature became Son of Man, our Brother, that we 'sons of men' (which of course includes daughters) might become 'sons of God' by grace - in him and through union with him. As the apostle puts it, 'God sent the Spirit of his Son into our hearts, the Spirit who cries out "Abba, Father" (Gal 4:6) - so that, whether we be Jews or Gentiles, through Christ 'we both have access to the Father by one Spirit' (Eph 2:18) in a life of what John Baillie used to call 'mediated immediacy'.

In the language of Athanasius and the Cappadocian divines, there is a double movement - in Creation, Incarnation and union with Christ - (a) a God-humanward movement, from (*ek*) the Father, through (*dia*) the Son, in (*en*) the Spirit, and (b) a human-Godward movement, to the Father, through the Son, in the Spirit.

Because God has established a relationship for us between God and humanity in Christ, worship (as Calvin said of justification) is in Christ as well as through Christ. We participate in Christ's worship of the Father by life in the Spirit, in virtue of what Christ has done and is doing for us. Or as Jungmann puts it in his great work *The Place of Christ in Liturgical Prayer*, our worship is not just *dia Christon*, because of the work and merits of Christ, but *dia Christou* - through the Person of Christ himself. We draw near to God our Father in and through the Mediator, our great High Priest - drawn by the Spirit of love. This is the way in which the Triune God in wonderful grace lifts us up into the life and love and communion of the Godhead.

In liturgical prayer, therefore, Christ has a dual role, enshrined in the mystery of the Incarnation. He is at once the God whom we worship and to whom we pray - 'Even so come, Lord Jesus' (Rev 22.10) - and he is at the same time the One who himself for us lived a life in the power of prayer, that we might find salvation and be restored to that communion with God for which we were created. There is thus a double purpose enshrined in the Nicene statement, 'Who for us men and our salvation came down from heaven... and was made man'. God in love gives himself to the world in Christ as God to be the Object of our love and worship, and at the same time he comes as Man to provide for us that life of human love and obedience and worship for which we were made and so constitute himself our Saviour.

It is important to preserve this recognition of the double role of Christ in worship, for as Jungmann has shown, fear of Arianism after Nicaea too often led the Church to play down the thought of the praying Christ, and onesidedly emphasise the rôle of the divine Christ as the Object of prayer. But when this happens, the tendency is for the priesthood of the Church to replace the Priesthood of Christ. The doctrine of the vicarious humanity of Christ in worship begins to disappear. We can understand therefore why Calvin was so concerned to recover the doctrine of the sole Priesthood of Christ - to put the true Priesthood back where it belongs in the humanity of Jesus - and to reinterpret the Church in corporate terms as a royal priesthood participating in the Priesthood of Christ, and to understand the Eucharist this way.

Fundamental to this Nicene model - this understanding of worship in terms of the vicarious humanity of Christ - are different considerations, based on biblical insights. I now select a few.

The One and the Many

In old Israel, the high priest represented Yahweh (God) to Israel and Israel to Yahweh in his own person. The covenant between Yahweh and Israel was focused in the person of the high priest and in the person of the king. It is this thought that lies behind the New Testament and patristic understanding of the inclusive and representative humanity of Christ, the Mediator of the New Covenant, who represents God to humanity and humanity to God in his own Person as the One on behalf of the Many.

This thought of the one and the many emerges out of the consciousness of Israel that she was chosen from among the nations to be a royal priesthood, a holy nation, a worshipping people, the recipient of God's grace for humankind. To this end she was called out of Egypt as God's son, and this thought of the one for the many was written deeply in the liturgical practices and sacrificial life of old Israel and interpreted like the Passover in terms of the memory of their redemption and Exodus from Egypt. The firstborn son symbolised this vicarious rôle and in turn the tribe of Levi was elected as the one tribe to act for the many (for all the sons of Israel), until in the fullness of time God sent his own Son to be the true Israel, and elect Servant, the true Priest, the firstborn of all creation, in whom and through whom God's purposes for all humanity might be brought to fulfilment.

In old Israel, as in Israel to this day, the great central act of Jewish worship took place on the Day of Atonement, the *yom kippur*. That was the day in the year which gathered up the worship of every other day. On that day an offering was made which gathered up all the other offerings made daily in the sanctuary, and on that day the worship of all Israel was led by one man, the high priest. Think for a moment of the symbolism of that day. The high priest stands before the people as their divinely appointed representative, bone of their bone, flesh of their flesh, their brother, in solidarity with the people he represents. All that he does, he does in their name. This is symbolised by the fact that he bears their names engraved on his breastplate and shoulders as a memorial before God (Ex 39:7). He consecrates himself for this ministry by certain liturgical acts of washing and sacrifice. Then comes the great moment when he takes an animal, lays his hands on the victim and vicariously confesses the aims of all Israel in an act of vicarious penitence acknowledging the just judgments of God; when the victim is immolated as a symbol of God's judgement, he takes the blood in a vessel, ascends into the Holy of Holies, and there vicariously intercedes for all Israel that God will remember his covenant promises and graciously forgive. He then returns to the waiting people outside with the Aaronic blessing of peace.

The Ministry of Christ Symbolised

The New Testament writers saw this as a foreshadowing of the ministry of Christ, who comes from God to be the true Priest, bone of our bone, flesh of our flesh, in solidarity with all humanity, all races, all colours, bearing on his divine heart the names, the needs, the sorrows, the injustices of all nations, to offer that worship, that obedience, that life of love to the Father which we cannot offer. In our Lord's high priestly prayer, where he intercedes for his people, he says, 'For them I sanctify myself, that they too may be truly sanctified' (John 17:19) - the One for the Many. 'Both the one who makes men holy and those who are made holy are of the same family. So Jesus is not ashamed to call them brothers' (Heb 2:11). Jesus' whole life of prayer and obedience and love, his whole life in the Spirit, is his self-consecration for us, for he offers, not an animal, but himself in death that he might be the Lamb of God to take away the sin of the world, saying Amen in our humanity to the just judgments of God, not to appease an angry God to condition him into being gracious, but in perfect acknowledgement of the love of God for a sinful world - to seal God's covenant purposes for humanity by his blood.

On Easter day, he says to Mary, '....I am returning to my Father and your Father, to my God and your God' (John 20:17). The High Priest is on his way into the Holy of Holies, to intercede for his people. Then the same day at evening, as the disciples are met in prayer, in an upper room, comes Jesus and says, 'Peace be with you' (John 20:19). It is the return of the High Priest, who now gives the gift of the Spirit that we may share with him his apostolic mission to the world (John 20:21-23).

When we think of the symbolism of the liturgy of old Israel on the Day of Atonement, we can make a twofold statement.

(a) When the high priest entered into the holy presence of Yahweh in the sanctuary, that he might present all Israel in his person to God, we can say, as Calvin puts it in his commentary (on Hebrews 6:19), all Israel entered in his person.

(b) Conversely, when he vicariously confessed their sins, and interceded for them before God, God accepted them as his forgiven people in the person of their high priest.

That double statement expresses the thought that God's covenant dealings with Israel were established at the hands of a mediator. In analogous fashion, we can make a twofold statement about Christ, in the light of the New Testament.

(a) When Jesus was born for us at Bethlehem, was baptised by the Spirit in Jordan, suffered under Pontius Pilate, rose again and ascended, we were born again, baptised by the Spirit, suffered, died, rose again and ascended in him, and now he presents us in himself to the Father as God's dear children, and our righteousness is hid with Christ in God - ready to be revealed at the last day.

(b) Conversely, because Jesus has lived our life, offered himself through the eternal Spirit without spot to the Father in our name and on our behalf, as the One for the Many, God accepts us in him. We are accepted in the Beloved Son.

Worship In as well as Through Christ

This means we worship the Father in Christ as well as through Christ, en Christo as well as dia Christou. Jesus is the Mediator of the New Covenant, the One in whom God draws near to humanity, and the One in whom we can draw near to God through the Spirit. We worship 'in the name of Christ' because he has already in our name made the one true offering to God, and because he ever lives to intercede for us in our name. The Covenant between God and humanity is concentrated in his Person.

This thought of the inclusive humanity of Christ, is thus not just 'Greek realism', the Platonic concept of the Ideal Man - how the Greeks understood 'the one and the many'. If it were, then the important thing would be not Jesus as an individual, but the Ideal, the Principle he embodied. It is rather the thoroughly non-dualistic biblical thought of Jesus being not only a man but the Man in whom God has given himself to the world and for the world, that his purposes for humanity might be brought to fulfilment.

It is this latter thought which was developed by Irenaeus in his doctrine of 'recapitulation' in terms of which, like Justin Martyr before him, he attacked Marcion's attempt to distinguish between the Creator God of the Old Testament and the Redeemer God of the New. The Christ by whom all things were made is the same

Christ as the One who 'for us men and our salvation was made man'. In other words the Son of God who created Adam for sonship, communion and immortality, does not abandon his loving purposes for humanity, but in order to redeem humanity himself becomes man, that he might fulfil for us in his own person God's purposes of love and obedience and worship. Thus what is lost 'in Adam' - communion with God - is restored and fulfilled for us in Christ and held out to us by the Spirit in the Lord's Supper. This of course is the Pauline doctrine of Romans chapter five and Ephesians chapter one, God's great purpose 'to bring all things in heaven and on earth together under one head, even Christ' (Eph 1:10).

This concept of recapitulation, of the fulfilment of God's purposes for humanity in and through the inclusive and vicarious humanity of Christ, was to receive fuller elaboration at the hands of Athanasius and the Cappadocian divines in the statement that 'the unassumed is the unredeemed'. In his book *On the Incarnation*, Athanasius asks what it means to speak of Christ as the Great Physician of our humanity. Christ does not heal us by standing over against us, diagnosing our sickness, prescribing medicine for us to take, and then going away, to leave us to get better by obeying his instructions - as an ordinary doctor might. No, he becomes the patient! He assumes that very humanity which is in need of redemption, and by being anointed by the Spirit in our humanity, by a life of perfect obedience, by dying and rising again for us, our humanity is healed in him. We are not just healed 'through Christ' because of the work of Christ but 'in and through Christ'. That was why these fathers did not hesitate to say, as Edward Irving the Scottish theologian in the early nineteenth century and Karl Barth in our own day have said, that Christ assumed 'fallen humanity' that our humanity might be turned back to God in him by his sinless life in the Spirit, and, through him, in us.

The God-humanward and the human-Godward relationship are both freely given to us in Jesus Christ

When we considered the 'Existential Model' of worship, we noticed that the God-humanward movement of grace is given to us in Christ, in virtue of which we are summoned to respond in faith, in decision, in repentance and obedience. But the weakness is that the only movement human-Godward is ours! In other words it does not do full justice to the meaning of grace, for it short-circuits the vicarious humanity of Christ. Grace does not only mean that in the coming of Jesus Christ, God gives himself in holy love to humanity. It also means the coming of God as man, to do for us as a human being what we cannot do for ourselves, to present us in himself through the eternal Spirit to the Father. In other words, the human-Godward movement, in which we are graciously given to participate, is given freely and unconditionally. Our response in faith and obedience is a response to the Response already made for us by Christ to the Father's holy love, a response we are summoned to make in union with Christ. This it seems to me was the great insight of the Greek fathers like Cyril of Alexandria, and which was elaborated by John Calvin in the Institutes in his exposition of grace in terms of the twin doctrines that 'all parts of our salvation are already complete in Christ' in virtue of his obedience for us, and that we are summoned to a life of 'union with Christ' to become in ourselves what we already are in Christ our Head.

Few distinctions in theology and pastoral counselling are more important than that discussed by Calvin in Book Three of the Institutes, between what he calls 'legal repentance' and 'evangelical repentance' in his critique of the medieval sacrament of penance. Legal repentance is the view that says, 'Repent, and IF you repent you will be forgiven!' as though God our Father has to be conditioned into being gracious. It makes the imperatives of obedience prior to the indicatives of grace, and regards God's love and acceptance and forgiveness as conditional upon what we do - upon our meritorious acts of repentance. Calvin argued that this inverted the evangelical order of grace, and made repentance prior to forgiveness, whereas in the New Testament forgiveness is logically prior to repentance. Evangelical repentance on the other hand takes the form that, 'Christ has borne your sins on the Cross, therefore repent!' That is, repentance is our response to grace, not a condition of grace. The good news of the Gospel is that 'There is forgiveness with God that he might be feared' and that he has spoken that word of forgiveness in Christ on the Cross - but that word summons from us a response of faith and penitence.

Legal and Evangelical Repentance

What did Calvin mean by saying that forgiveness is logically prior to repentance? The point is of fundamental importance in our interpersonal relationships. If two people have the misfortune to have a quarrel, and then one day one comes to the other and says, in all sincerity, 'I forgive you!' it is clear that that is not only a word of love and reconciliation, but also a word (perhaps a withering word) of condemnation - for in pronouncing his forgiveness, he is clearly implying that the other person is the guilty party! Indeed it can be a very hurtful thing, if not a self-righteous thing, to say to someone, 'I forgive you!' How would the other person be likely to react? I could imagine that his immediate reaction would be one of indignation. Sensing the element of judgement, of condemnation in his word, he might well reject the forgiveness, because he refuses to submit to the verdict of guilty implied in it. He would be 'impenitent' - there would be no 'change of heart'. But supposing on subsequent reflection, he comes back to his friend and says, 'You were quite right! I was in the wrong!', implicit in his acceptance of love and forgiveness, he would be submitting to the verdict of guilty. There would be a real change of mind, an act of penitence on his part.

So it is with the Gospel of the Incarnation. God in Christ has spoken to the world his word of forgiveness, his word of love which is at the same time his word of judgement and condemnation. But implicit in our receiving the word of the Cross, the word of the Father's love, there is, on our part, a humble submission to the verdict of guilty. That lies at the heart of the Reformation understanding of grace. But who can make that perfect response of love, that perfect act of penitence, that perfect submission to the verdict of guilty? What we cannot do, God has done for us in Christ.

It was that insight which John McLeod Campbell, the Scottish theologian, developed in his remarkable, but often misunderstood book, *The Nature of the Atonement*, where he expounded this doctrine of vicarious repentance - vicarious evangelical repentance - in terms of the vicarious humanity and Sonship of Christ. He grasped vividly the thought that in the New Testament witness to Christ, we discern a God-humanward movement and a human-Godward movement, that, as he puts it, Christ deals with humanity on the part of God and deals with God on behalf of humanity. In Jesus Christ the incarnate Son of the Father, we have both God giving himself to humanity in unconditional forgiveness, and at the same time we see Jesus, as the representative Head of the race, in his life of filial obedience, saying Amen in our humanity to the just judgement of God - not only vicariously confessing our sin, as our Great High Priest and Intercessor, but submitting for us (not for himself) to the verdict of guilty, in offering his life in death on the Cross. Christ has once and for all made the perfect Response of vicarious evangelical repentance to the Father's love and the Father's judgement for us, and now by the Spirit unites us with himself that we might live a life of love and intercession and daily penitence before the Cross.

Campbell saw clearly that God does not merely speak his Word of forgiveness and then throw us back on ourselves to make our response of repentance - even of evangelical repentance! God knows our weaknesses and impotence. Grace means that in Jesus Christ we have God personally present as Man giving himself in forgiveness, and at the same time from our side vicariously making the perfect Response for us to that Word. We are certainly summoned unconditionally to a life of faith and repentance, but our response of evangelical repentance is now by the grace of God, through the Spirit, a response to a Response - our response to the Word of the Cross - made in virtue of our union with Christ.

McLeod Campbell grasped clearly what this means for theology, that we must interpret atonement in terms of the Incarnation, and not the Incarnation in terms of atonement. If, therefore, he said, we consider long and carefully Who Christ is, and look long at his whole life of filial obedience and perfect sympathy culminating on the Cross, then alone can we begin to understand something of the nature of the atoning act by which we are reconciled to God. In the vicarious life and death of Jesus of Nazareth - in his perfect humanity - we see both the heart of God laid bare to humanity in holy love - not only in words of unfathomable love but also of withering exposure of our human sin and pretensions - and at the same time we see in that human life culminating in death, a life of perfect sonship and a life of humble costly submission to the verdict of guilty on a sinful world.

But that life of vicarious sonship and penitence must be interpreted for the here and now, not just the past. Jesus received the Word of forgiveness for us from the Father, not only that our past sins might be wiped out, but in order that we might receive the Spirit of adoption, and be restored to the status of sonship by a life of union with Christ - that we might be brought to joyful evangelical repentance.

'Christ in our Place' and 'Sharing in Christ' are twin doctrines which must not be separated

As Christ was anointed by the Spirit in our humanity to fulfil his ministry for us, so we are united by the same Spirit to share his ministry. In the New Testament, Christ is presented as uniting us with himself in his twofold ministry of bringing God to humanity and humanity to God. Correspondingly there is a two-fold ministry of the Spirit. There is a God-humanward movement of the Spirit, in creating, in revealing, in renewing us in worship, in giving gifts to the Church. But there is also a human-Godward ministry of the Spirit of leading us to the Father through Christ - *dia Christou* - where 'the Spirit himself intercedes for us' (Rom 8:26) lifting us up into communion with God, into the very life of the Triune God. He is both speaking Spirit and interceding Spirit, with a prophetic and a priestly office. Thus the vicarious humanity of Christ and the vicarious priestly work of the Spirit are both fundamental for our understanding of worship, where Christ our Brother, our Advocate, our High Priest, units us with himself in his Self-presentation on our behalf to the Father.

'Participation' is thus a vital word. It holds together what WE do, and that in which we are given to participate - the Son's communion with the Father, and the Son's mission from the Father to the world.

In this chapter, James Torrance has many references, which can be found in chapter six of The Incarnation, *edited by T.F. Torrance and published by the Handsel Press*

Stoking the Fire

1 What is wrong with the idea that worship is something we do with the help of the minister? What practical consequence does such a theology of worship have?

2 What is freeing about understanding our worship as participating in the incarnate Son's communion with the Father?

3 When Harnack separated the reality of Christ's incarnation from the principle, or idea, of his sacrificial love, what happened to his Christianity? What would worship based on such a theology look like?

4 In the existential model of worship, the focus is on the immediacy of our faith experience. What is the dangerous flaw in this view?

5 In the Nicene model of worship, what is the dual role that Christ enacts?

6 In Israel, on the Day of Atonement, in what ways did the High Priest act vicariously for the people? In what ways does Jesus, in his actions as our High Priest, parallel the actions of the Day of Atonement?

7 The church fathers used the expression 'the unassumed is the unredeemed'. How did Athanasius explain this through a medical illustration?

8 In what way is our response to God's grace 'a response to a Response'?

I Know Not How To Pray

Words by James B. Torrance
Music by Christine Dieckmann

I know not how to pray, O Lord. So weak and frail am I.

Lord Je- sus to Your out - stretched arms in love I dai - ly fly:

For You have prayed for me.

2. I know not how to pray, O Lord,
O'erwhelmed by grief am I --
Lord Jesus, in Your wondrous love
You hear my anxious cry
And ever pray for me.

3. I Know not how to pray, O Lord,
For, full of tears and pain,
I groan, yet in my soul I know
My cry is not in vain,
O teach me how to pray.

4. Although I know not how to pray,
Your spirit intercedes,
Convincing me of pardoned sin;
For me in love He pleads
And teaches me to pray.

5. O take my worthless sighs and fears
And make my prayers Your own.
O put Your prayer within my lips
And lead me to God's throne,
That I may love like You.

6. O draw me to your Father's heart,
Lord Jesus, when I pray
And whisper in my troubled ear,
"Your sins are washed away;
Come home with Me today."

7. At home within our Father's house,
Your Father, Lord - and mine -
I'm lifted up by Your embrace
To share in love divine,
Which floods my heart with joy.

8. Transfigured by Your glory, Lord,
Renewed in heart and mind,
I'll sing angelic songs of praise
With joy which all can find
In You alone, O Lord.

9. I'll love You, O my Father God,
Through Jesus Christ, Your Son,
I'll love you in the Spirit, Lord,
In whom we all are one,
Made holy by Your love.

Ignition Points

We are given the Spirit to participate in the Son's communion with the Father. The doctrine of the Trinity is thus the grammar of our understanding of prayer and communion. To this end we have been created as men and women in the image of God to find our true being in a life of prayer and communion.

We know we ought to pray, we try to pray, but we fail. We do not know how to pray. But God so loves us and longs to draw us into a life of loving communion that he comes to us in Christ to stand in for us, to pray for us and with us and in us, sending the Spirit of his Son into our hearts crying 'Abba, Father!'

The Son of God takes our humanity, sanctifies it by his vicarious life in the Spirit, carries it to the grave to be crucified and buried in him, and in his resurrection and ascension carries it into the holy presence of God.

Grace is God freely and personally giving himself to us in covenant love in Jesus Christ to draw us by his Holy Spirit to bind us to himself in loving fellowship. God's grace is 'unconditionally free.'

In prayer we look away to God our Father, to Jesus Christ our High Priest, as he intercedes for us, with us and in us, trusting in his grace to hear and answer our prayers, yielding, surrendering our wills to his will.

We are summoned all our life to look away in faith to Christ our High Priest, to let him lift us up daily by the Spirit into his prayer life. Faith means surrendering ourselves, abandoning ourselves daily to be led by the Spirit.

Chapter Four

PRAYER AND THE PRIESTHOOD OF CHRIST

James B. Torrance

The vicarious humanity of Christ extends to the inmost part of us. Christ takes our place even in the very intimacy of prayer. James Torrance shows us how this is a tremendous relief. As he says, we want to pray, we try to pray, but we fail. The gospel directs us then to look away from ourselves and to Jesus. 'In our name, on our behalf, in a human body, Jesus lived a life of prayer, a life in the Spirit in communion with the Father.' Now he gives us to share in his life of prayer. In Jesus, by the power of the Holy Spirit, we are drawn into prayer that is a wonderful communion in the love of the Triune God. Prayer becomes not what we do - in our harried and exhausted effort - but what Christ does in us and for us. This is the exhilarating freedom of the gospel!

The story is told about D.L. Moody, the American evangelist, that on one of his visits to Scotland he addressed a gathering of several hundred schoolchildren in Glasgow, and put a question to them which he had frequently put to children across the world: 'What is prayer?' To his astonishment, nearly every single hand went up. They all knew the same answer, from the old Westminster *Shorter Catechism* which they had been taught at school.

Prayer is an offering up of our desires unto God, for things agreeable to his will, in the name of Christ, with confession of our sins, and thankful acknowledgement of his mercies.

Some of us were taught that at school. But I wonder how many understood the meaning of that classical statement. I am sure I did not at that age. I learned more about prayer then at my mother's knee or in the context of family prayers.

We can only pray *in the name of Christ* because Christ has already in our name, offered up our desires to God and continues to offer them. In our name he lived a life in the Spirit agreeable to the will of God. In our name and in our place he vicariously confessed our sins and submitted for us to the verdict of guilty on the Cross, taking the condemnation of our sins to himself (the 'curse', the 'wrath of God' in New Testament terms) and in our name gave thanks to God. We pray 'in the name of Christ' because of what Christ *has already* done for us, and is doing for us *today* in our name, on our behalf.

This finds vivid expression in what the New Testament says about the *Priesthood of Christ* in his ministry of prayer and intercession, as in our Lord's high priestly prayer in John 17 and in the Epistle to the Hebrews. 'Because Jesus lives forever, he has a permanent priesthood. Therefore he is able to save completely all who come to God through Him, because he always lives to intercede for them' (Heb 7:24-25). The New Testament writers use the liturgical symbolism of the priesthood in old Israel to interpret the ministry of Jesus, and not least his prayer life.

In old Israel, as in Israel to this day, the central act of worship and prayer took place on the Day of Atonement (*yom kippur*). That was the day in the year which gathered up the worship and prayers of every other day. On that day an offering was made to God which gathered up every other offering made daily in the sanctuaries. On that day, the worship and prayers of all Israel were led by one man, the high priest, 'the one on behalf of the many'. I have discussed this in my chapter on 'The Meaning of Worship' (see p. 44). The great climax came when the high priest, with the names of all Israel on his breastplate and shoulder, laid his hands on the head of an animal and sacrificed it, vicariously confessing the sins of all Israel, acknowledging the just judgments of God. He then took the blood of the sacrificial victim in a vessel, 'ascended' into the Holy of Holies and there interceded for all Israel that God would remember his covenant promises and forgive his people. As he was praying in the holy presence of God, all Israel was praying outside, one great volume of prayer ascending to God, led by the high priest. He then returned to the waiting people outside with the Aaronic blessing of peace. 'The Lord said to Moses, "Tell Aaron and his sons: 'This is how you are to bless the Israelites. Say to them: The Lord bless you and keep you. The Lord make his face shine upon you and be gracious to you; the Lord turn his face toward you and give you peace.' So they will *put my name* on the Israelites and I will bless them.'" (Num 6:22-27). As a mediator, he represented God to Israel and Israel to God in his ministry.

Israel's worship was an ordinance of grace, their God given response to grace. When the high priest made his sacrifice and sprinkled the blood of the victim on the ark of the covenant on 'the propitiatory' in the Holy of Holies, he was not seeking to placate an angry God as in pagan worship! Their worship was a God-given response to grace, the acknowledgement that God is gracious and propitious, and so in intercession the high priest calls on God to remember his promises to his covenant people. He is a covenant God of love and grace, not a 'contract-god' who has to be conditioned into being gracious! Their worship was a response to grace, not 'a condition' of grace. The word *kipper* in the Old Testament, 'to propitiate, to cover' is never used with man as the agent placating an angry God as in pagan worship but is used of God providing for Israel in this liturgical act a witness to his grace that he is propitious, that symbolically the 'condemnation' of their sins is taken away.

The New Testament writers saw this as the foreshadowing of the mediatorial ministry of Christ, who brings God's Word of grace and forgiveness to the world, and who in our name and on our behalf offered his life in loving obedience to the Father as the propitiation for the sins of the world (1 John 2:1-2) and returns in the power of the Spirit to bless us, to cleanse us, to draw us into his communion with the Father and share his intercessions. This again is the significance of the teaching of Jesus in the Upper Room on the eve of the Cross, when he says: 'In that day (i.e. in the future, when the Spirit comes) you may ask for anything *in my name*, and I will do it.' 'My Father will give you whatever you ask *in my name*.' (John 14:14, 16:23). In total, six times our Lord speaks about praying 'in my name' and six times he says 'whatever you ask' or 'anything' you ask for. He is going to make the only sacrifice which will wipe out sin and lead them into the Holy of Holies, where he intercedes for us in the presence of the Father.

This is the good news of the Gospel. In our name, on our behalf, in a human body, Jesus lived a life of prayer, a life in the Spirit in communion with the Father, to sanctify our humanity. He carried our old humanity in himself to the grave that our old humanity might be buried in the garden of Joseph of Arimathea and renewed in him. He rises from the dead, the first of a new creation, ascends now as our great High Priest to live for us in our humanity, in a glorified humanity, an eternal life of communion with the Father, to intercede for us 'in the Holy of Holies', 'in heavenly places'. But he does not do that alone. He pours out his Spirit on the Church at Pentecost to lift us up into that life of communion with the Father that we might participate in his glorified life, in his prayers, his intercessions, his mission to the world. The important New Testament word *koinonia* can be translated by communion, fellowship, sharing, participating, having in common with Christ. That is the message of the New Testament, the secret of our prayer life. Our great High Priest has entered for us sinful men and women into the Holy of Holies, having made sacrifice for our sins, and now intercedes for us within the veil. He does not leave us outside as the high priest had to do in old Israel on the Day of Atonement but he takes us with himself by the Holy Spirit into the Holy of Holies leading us by the Holy Spirit to the Father. Therefore we have to hold two things together. First, he has *already* taken our humanity into the Holy of Holies, the presence of the Father in his own person. Second, he comes to us *today* by the Holy Spirit to take us with him into the Holiest of All, to present us 'without stain or wrinkle or any other blemish' to the Father (Eph 5:27).

Here we see the nature of the Church as 'a chosen people, a royal priesthood, a holy nation, a people belonging to God' (1 Peter 2:9ff.) - *holy in Christ*, participating by the Holy Spirit in the Incarnate Son's communion with the Father - 'made holy through the sacrifice of the body of Jesus Christ once and for all' (Heb 10:10). That is the Trinitarian nature of prayer and of the Church, as it was baptised into Christ at Pentecost. In the ten days between the Ascension and the Day of Pentecost, the disciples, with Mary, our Lord's mother, other women and his brothers, and one hundred and twenty of the followers of Jesus, were met with one accord, in one place, in supplication and in prayer for the Spirit, and in answer to prayer, the Spirit came as Jesus had promised (John 14:16; 16:7ff.; Luke 24:49; Acts 1:4,5, ch.2). There comes a very significant verse in Peter's sermon (Acts 2:33) when he refers to the Ascension of our Lord and the fulfilment of Jesus' promise: 'Exalted to the right hand of God, he has received from the Father the promised Holy

Spirit and has poured out what you now see and hear'. It is as though Jesus began his earthly ministry by being baptised by the Holy Spirit for us in the waters of Jordan and now commences his heavenly ministry by baptising the Church with the Holy Spirit at Pentecost, to participate with him in his life of communion with the Father, and in his mission to the world. So the writer to the Hebrews says: 'Therefore, holy brothers, who share in the heavenly calling, fix your thoughts on Jesus, the apostle and high priest whom we confess' (Heb 3:1).

The Church, as the Body of Christ, has four foundations or cornerstones:

1   *The Divinity of Christ.* The Son of God is conceived by the Holy Spirit in the womb of the Virgin Mary, 'God with us'.

2   *The Incarnation,* the real humanity of Christ. Mary bears a human child. God assumes our humanity in the womb of Mary, that our fallen humanity might be sanctified by the Spirit *in Him.*

3   *The Atonement on the Cross.* Christ carries our old humanity in himself to the grave. We thus judge that when Christ died for all, we died in him. 'How much more, then, will the blood of Christ, who through the eternal Spirit offered himself unblemished to God, cleanse our consciences from acts that lead to death, so that we may serve the living God!' (Heb 9:14).

4   *The Resurrection and Ascension* to the throne of God, where he carries our humanity, sanctified in himself into the Holy of Holies, to reign as our Royal Priest (cf. Psalm 110).

The Ascension is the glorious fruit of all that goes before. The Holy Spirit was sent down after the Ascension. It is as if the whole purpose of the Incarnation, Death, Resurrection and Ascension, is in order that we might receive the Holy Spirit, that the Triune God of grace might bring to fulfilment the purposes of creation in sanctifying our humanity in Christ, that we might be brought into a life of holy communion, a life of prayer. Our great High Priest who is interceding for us, comes to us by the Spirit to pray with us and in us and lead us in our prayers. 'Since we have a great High Priest over the house of God, let us draw near to God with a sincere heart in full assurance of faith' (Heb 10:21-22).

Therefore we can say three things about the prayer life:

1   Jesus Christ intercedes for us. He stands in for us as the ascended Lord, the High Priest in the Holiest of All.

2   He gives us the Holy Spirit (Acts 2:33).

3   He unites us with himself in prayer, to participate in his prayers and communion with the Father. He draws us into a 'prayer union' that we might again 'abide in him', the true Vine.

To have a proper understanding of the Church as a royal priesthood, we need to stress two things:

1   *First, the Trinitarian nature of prayer.*

God is *love* and love in God implies communion between the Persons. The Father loves the Son in the communion of the Holy Spirit. The Son loves the Father in the communion of the Holy Spirit. God has his being in loving communion. We have been created and redeemed in Christ to participate by the Holy Spirit in that life of communion with God and with one another - that communion which is in God. We are given the Spirit to participate in the Son's communion with the Father. The doctrine of the Trinity is thus the grammar of our understanding of prayer and communion. To this end we have been created as men and women in the image of God to find our true being in a life of prayer and communion.

2   *Second, the Church lives and prays by grace alone.*

St Paul in his letter to the Romans where he expounds becoming right and holy by grace alone, says of prayer: 'In the same way, the Spirit helps us in our weakness. We do not know what we ought to pray, but the Spirit himself intercedes for us with groans that words cannot express. And he who searches our hearts knows the mind of the Spirit, because the Spirit intercedes for the saints in accordance with God's will' (Rom 8:26-27). We know we ought to pray, we try to pray, but we fail. We do not know how to pray. But God so loves us and longs to draw us into a life of loving communion that he comes to us in Christ to stand in for us, to pray for us and with us and in us, sending the Spirit of his Son into our hearts crying 'Abba, Father' (Rom 8:15; Gal 4:6).

Here is the significance of what theologians call *the vicarious humanity of Christ* - of 'Christ in our place' - of the Triune God coming in Jesus Christ to stand in for us, to do for us and in us by the Holy Spirit what we cannot do for ourselves, to bring his purposes for us to fulfilment in our humanity.

This is the heart of the Pauline message of justification by faith in the Epistles to the Romans and to the Galatians. We are all under the righteous requirements (*dikaiomata*) of the law. We try to fulfil it, but we fail and fall under the condemnation (*katakrimata*) of the law. Does God then abandon his righteous purposes for us? No! In love he sends his Son to be born of a woman under the law to redeem us from the curse (*katara*) of the law, that we might receive the adoption of sons. Because we are sons, God has sent the Spirit of his Son into our hearts, the Spirit who calls out 'Abba, Father' (Gal 4:4-6). The righteous requirements (*dikaiomata*) of the law are thus, by grace alone, fulfilled for us by Christ and in us by the Spirit, as we walk not after the flesh (with a false self confidence in ourselves) but after the Spirit. There is thus no condemnation for those who are in Christ (Rom 8:1-4).

What Paul says about righteousness, he goes on at once to say about prayer. The Triune God has created us for a life of worship and prayer, under the 'regulations of worship' (*dikaiomata latreias*, Heb 9:1) for a life of wonderful communion. But try as we might to fulfil these regulations, we cannot, we fail: 'the prescribed offerings and sacrifices cannot give the worshipper a clear conscience' (Heb 9:9). So Paul says, as we have seen, 'We do not know how to pray as we ought, but the Spirit intercedes for us with groans which words cannot express and he who searches our hearts knows the mind of the Spirit, because the Spirit intercedes for us' (Rom 8:26-27). The apostle then goes on to say about prayer: 'Who is he that condemns?' - when we feel under condemnation for our failure in the prayer life. 'Christ Jesus who died... who was raised to life, is at the right hand of God and is also interceding for us. Who then shall separate us from the love of Christ?' (Rom 8:34-35). This is the New Testament teaching about the Priesthood of Christ. God in grace comes as man to stand in for us in our prayer life.

Again, what the New Testament says about righteousness and prayer, it says of *holiness*. The command of God is: 'Be holy because I am holy' (1 Pet 1:16). But none of us can make ourselves holy. But in grace God comes to stand in for us in Jesus Christ, that he might bring us into 'the Holy of Holies', into holy communion with our Father. The Son of God takes our humanity, sanctifies it by his vicarious life in the Spirit (John 17:17-18), carries it to the grave to be crucified and buried in him, and in his resurrection and ascension carries it into the holy presence of God. 'And by that will, we have been made holy through the sacrifice of the body of Jesus Christ once for all' (Heb 10:10). 'We are holy and blameless' (*sancti et immaculati*) in him (Eph 1:4), and now given the Holy Spirit and called to be holy in ourselves. We believe one, holy, catholic and apostolic Church. The Church is holy and immaculate *in Christ* and called to be holy in herself by life in the Spirit. Only so can we raise holy hands to the Lord in prayer.

What we have said about righteousness, prayer and holiness, we can say of almost all our doctrines, not least our calling to be a 'royal priesthood'. God has created us in his image to be 'the priests of creation', and called Israel to be a royal priesthood on behalf of the world. But Israel failed - we all fail. But does God abandon his purposes for creation? In grace, he comes to stand in for us in Christ - in a twofold way. Christ as our great High Priest made atonement for our sins once and for all upon the Cross. But also as our eternal priest, 'after the order of Melchizedek', he has a permanent priesthood, and ever lives to intercede for us as we come to God through him (Heb ch.7). Too often we have stressed the once and for all priesthood of Christ on the Cross but neglected the continuing priesthood of Christ. He not only made the once and for all *sin offering* on the Cross to be the propitiation for our sins, but he presents us with our prayers in himself to the Father as God's dear children, his brothers and sisters, in his *thank offering*. For a proper understanding of the Church, of our worship and our prayers, we need a proper understanding of grace. We need to contemplate the Triune God of Grace who has come to us in Christ, to be our Brother, to stand in for us, to bring to fulfilment for us and in us, by the Holy Spirit, his Triune purposes of love, for Israel, for the Church, for the world. He calls us to a life of prayer and intercession 'in the name of Christ'.

In the light of all this, what can we say about our *prayer life*?

1   *We pray by Grace alone*

We do not know how to pray as we ought, but Christ prays for us, with us and in us. Prayer is the Father's gift of grace in giving us Christ to stand in for us and in giving us the Holy Spirit to teach us to pray, and lift us up in prayer into a life of loving communion. Grace is not a 'thing', an impersonal 'cause'. The Church has too often spoken about imparted grace, efficacious grace, created grace, invisible grace, infused grace in ways which can blur its personal nature. Grace is God freely and personally giving *himself* to us in covenant love in Jesus Christ to draw us by his Holy Spirit to bind us to himself in loving fellowship. God's grace is 'unconditionally free'. He is a covenant God not a 'contract-god'. We must not regard prayer as a legal duty we must fulfil *if* God is going to bless us! It is a joyful response of love to our Father. What kind of a human father would he be who says to his child: 'I shall only love you IF...!'? There is no such thing as conditional love in God or in humanity. Too often we have read notions of 'contract' into the word 'Father', and created a 'religion' of good works which is not the gospel of grace. Our Lord was aware of the danger of reading false patriarchal concepts into the word 'father' when speaking of God (Matt 23:9-12; 11:27). He seeks to evacuate the word father of all such notions. We know the Father and his love by looking at Jesus Christ as he takes the form of a servant on the Cross that we may become loving sons of a loving Father.

2 *We pray by faith alone*

In prayer, in our helplessness we look away to God our Father, to Jesus Christ our High Priest, as he intercedes for us, with us and in us, trusting in his grace to hear and answer our prayers, yielding, surrendering our wills to his will. This is beautifully expressed in the *Prayer of Abandonment* by Charles de Foucauld:

> Father, I abandon myself into your hands:
> Do with me what you will.
> Whatever you will do, I will thank you.
> Let only your will be done in me,
> As in all your creatures.
> And I'll ask nothing else, my Lord.
> Into your hands I commend my spirit:
> I give it to you with all the love of my heart
> For I love you Lord, and so need to give myself,
> To surrender myself into your hands
> With a trust beyond all measure,
> Because you are my Father.

It was in that spirit of faith and abandonment that Mary said: 'Behold the handmaid of the Lord: be it unto me according to your word'. That is also a beautiful picture of our Lord himself, marching to the Cross in the Garden of Gethsemane, surrendering himself to do our Father's will. That is the perfect model for the Church's prayer life. So when we pray: 'Thy will be done', we surrender ourselves, abandon ourselves in faith into the loving hands of God, believing he is faithful to his promises and will answer our prayers. As we pray in faith, Christ takes our prayers, cleanses them, makes them his prayers to the Father, presenting us in himself to the Father, and makes his prayers our prayers.

3 *We pray in the Spirit*

'The Spirit helps us in our weakness... the Spirit intercedes for the saints in accordance with God's will' (Rom 8:26-27). When we do not know how to pray as we ought, the Spirit comes to open our hearts in prayer and lead us in our intercessions. In Acts 1 and 2 as we saw, in the period between the Ascension and Pentecost, the disciples prayed for the coming of the Spirit, and the ascended Lord, as Peter said in his sermon (2:33) pours out the Spirit upon them, the Spirit he had received from the Father. They both prayed for the Spirit, and were moved by the Spirit to pray. The Spirit comes to the praying community, and creates a community of love and prayer (Acts 2:45ff.), a royal priesthood sharing in the intercessions of Christ. We do not only begin the Christian life by committing ourselves in faith to Jesus Christ, to receive the forgiveness of our sins. We are summoned all our life to look away in faith to Christ our High Priest, to let him lift us up daily by the Spirit into his prayer life. Faith means surrendering ourselves, abandoning ourselves daily to be led by the Spirit. The Epistle to the Hebrews was written to a church which had *begun* by looking to Jesus Christ and his Cross for the forgiveness of sins but then they drifted away from their faith in God and began, with a false confidence in the flesh, to rely on their own religious efforts and prayers and fell away. They were in danger of being like Israel of old who came rejoicing out of Egypt on the road to the promised land but then turned away from God, and perished in the wilderness. So the writer exhorts these Hebrew Christians to keep looking away from themselves in faith to Jesus Christ, their High Priest, to lead them on to the promised land. So Paul writes to the Church at Galatia to say: 'Having begun in the Spirit are you now made perfect in the flesh - by keeping the law?' We receive the Spirit by faith alone, by grace alone, not only at the beginning of our Christian lives but to the end. We can only pray aright in the Spirit who is given to us as we abandon ourselves daily to Christ who ever lives to intercede for us and with us.

4 *In prayer we are led into the Holy Presence of God*

Our High Priest leads us by the Holy Spirit into the Holy of Holies. 'Therefore, brothers, since we have confidence to enter the Most Holy Place by the blood of Jesus, by a new and living way opened for us through the curtain, that is, his body, and since we have a great priest over the house of God, let us draw near to God with a sincere heart in full assurance of faith...' (Heb 10:19-22). We do not make ourselves holy but we are holy in Christ sanctified by his Cross and by his Holy Spirit. So in our Lord's High Priestly prayer, he prayed: 'Holy Father, protect them by the power of your name. Sanctify them by the truth, your word is truth... For them I sanctify myself, that they too may be truly sanctified' (made holy - John 17:16-19). To this end, at the last Supper, Jesus promised the Holy Spirit, who came after his death, resurrection and ascension, to lead us into the holy presence of the Father in loving communion. In the Sermon on the Mount, Jesus said: 'When you pray, go into your room, close the door and pray to your Father in secret. Then your Father, who sees what is done in secret, will reward you.' (Matt 6:6). The Holy of Holies can be 'the inner closet' of our own hearts as we commune with our holy Father in prayer. So Paul writes to the Ephesians: 'Praise be to the God and Father of our Lord Jesus Christ who has blessed us in the heavenly realms with every spiritual blessing in Christ. For he chose us in him, before the foundation of the world, to be holy and blameless in him (Eph 1:3-4). 'Be holy because I am holy' (1 Pet 1:16). We are only holy in Christ, and only in him can we lift up holy hands to the Lord in prayer. 'Don't you know that you yourselves are God's temple and that God's Spirit lives in you?' (1 Cor 3:16). Our bodies are by God's grace the temple of the Holy Spirit - the sanctuary where prayer is offered in gratitude to God.

J. Jungmann, the Jesuit liturgical scholar, in his important work *The Place of Christ in Liturgical Prayer*, has shown that in the New Testament and in the liturgies of the early Church in the first three centuries, Christ was given a twofold role in Christian worship. On the one hand, prayer was offered to Jesus Christ as God. We pray to the Father and to the Son and to the Holy Spirit. But on the other hand, Jesus Christ was seen to be our great High Priest, as our brother man, praying to the Father, the one who intercedes for us and leads our praises and prayers, presenting us with them to the Father. Then at the time of the Arian-Nicene controversy, one of Arius' main arguments against the deity of Christ was that Jesus Christ could not be God because he was a man who prayed to God in the Gospel story, as at his baptism, on the mountainside, at the Last Supper, in Gethsemane and on the Cross. He cannot be both God and a man praying to God! Athanasius replied: 'Arius you do not understand the meaning of grace!' The God to whom we pray knows we want to pray, try to pray, but cannot pray, so comes to stand in for us as our brother man in Jesus Christ to pray for us and with us and lead us in our prayers. We pray by grace alone through the gift of Jesus Christ and the Holy Spirit. So Christ is very God, the God to whom we pray, and at the same time very man, the man who prays for us and with us our great High Priest. The Nicene Fathers, with their understanding of the place of Jesus Christ in worship and prayer, won the day as in the Nicene Creed. But Jungmann points out that fear of Arianism and the Arian argument - pitting the praying humanity of Jesus against the deity of Christ - led the Church, while stressing the deity of Christ, to play down the priesthood of Christ. What was the result? The Church, the *ecclesia*, took over the role of being the high priest for humanity, the mediator of grace, with the added vicarious role of Mary and the saints.

We can therefore understand the biblical emphasis of the Reformers like John Calvin and John Knox, in calling the Church back to the sole priesthood and kingship of Christ. Jesus Christ is both the object of our worship and prayer and the leader of our worship, as in the Epistle to the Hebrews. Calvin expounded this so clearly in his magnificent commentary on *Hebrews*. The Reformers therefore reinterpreted the Church as the royal priesthood that shares by grace in the priesthood of Christ. In spite of this Reformation emphasis, much Protestantism since has so stressed *our* worship and *our* prayers - 'the priesthood of all believers' - that it too can obscure the sole priesthood of Christ. While stressing the once and for all priesthood of Christ on the Cross, we can lose sight of the continuing priesthood of Christ, who ever lives to intercede for us and with us and in us, by speaking of prayer as what we do (no doubt in response to the Cross). We need to recover the Trinitarian nature of grace and prayer, that prayer is the gift of participating through the Spirit in the prayers of Jesus Christ the only mediator. 'I urge then, first of all, that requests, prayers, intercession and thanksgiving be made for everyone... this is good, and pleases God our Saviour, who wants all men to be saved and to come to a knowledge of the truth. For there is one God and one mediator between God and men, the man Christ Jesus, who gave himself as a ransom for all...' (1 Tim 2:1-6).

Stoking the Fire

1 What has happened to Christ's humanity since the ascension? What is he doing now?

2 What is the role of the Spirit in partnership with Christ's interceding for us?

3 How does God address through Christ our failure to pray as we ought?

4 What causes us to think of prayer as a 'legal duty'? And how does concentrating on the unconditional love of God in Christ transform prayer from duty to joy?

5 What is so essential about 'looking away from ourselves' and to Christ Jesus both in prayer and in the whole of the Christian life?

6 How is it that we pray both *to* Jesus and *with* Jesus?

7 Describe what James Torrance means by 'the Trinitarian nature of grace and prayer'.

Praying to the Father, through the Son, in the Spirit

'Christ Jesus is interceding for us' (Rom 8:34)

'He always lives to intercede for those who come to God through him' (Heb 7:25)

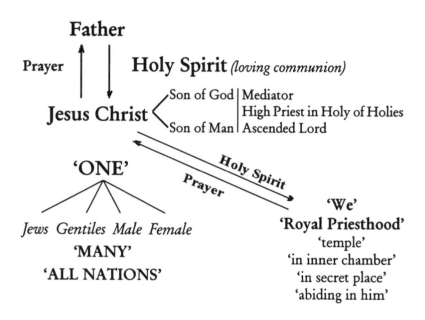

Father → Son
'You are my Son....'   'Ask of me and I will answer' (Ps 2:7-8)

Son → Father
'Father, I thank you that you always hear me' (John 11:41-42)

*Prayer - participating by the Holy Spirit
in the Son's communion with the Father
and the Son's mission from the Father to the world*

'Jesus - apostle and high priest' (Heb 3:1)

Ignition Points

Ministry can only rightly be shaped and determined by the ministry of Jesus Christ.

There is no other ministry acceptable to God and able to advance his Kingdom other than the ministry exercised by Jesus Christ.

The Church is called so to open her life to God and surrender herself to God that when she lives and ministers God himself in Christ lives, speaks and ministers in and through her and manifests himself to the world.

Try as we might, we are not able of ourselves to produce the love which alone can sustain, enthuse and fulfil our ministry. For love is a gift from God. We need to ask for it in prayer, not once nor twice, but every day.

In preaching and in pastoral ministry we dare not direct attention to ourselves, to our preaching or our oratory. If we do this, we will turn people's attention away from Christ and will hinder the work of the Gospel. Our aim must always be to direct attention to God in his Triune nature.

When we do not pray we are not following the example of Jesus nor sharing in his ministry and our people suffer.

Chapter Five
SHARING IN THE MINISTRY OF CHRIST

David W. Torrance

Years of pastoral experience undergird this gently compelling
essay. David Torrance communicates his love for the great
calling of the church, which is 'to represent God in his
ministry to the world... the Church is called so to open her
life to God and surrender herself to God that when she lives
and ministers, God himself in Christ lives, speaks and
ministers in and through her'. While this ministry 'belongs
to the whole church', David Torrance takes a particular look
at the work of the parish minister. Here, then, is a pastor's
heart unfurled as he calls his people to a life of deeper love,
prayer and compassion in every season of life. The essay is
filled with practical advice for lay and clergy alike.

When Jesus met with his disciples in the upper room on the evening
of the first day of resurrection, he said, 'Peace be with you! As the
Father has sent me, I am sending you'. And with that he breathed
on them and said, 'Receive the Holy Spirit. If you forgive anyone
his sins, they are forgiven; if you do not forgive them, they are not
forgiven' (John 20:21-23). From Jesus' commissioning of his
disciples, it is clear that the ministry of the Church is commanded
by God. This is in line with what he said shortly before his ascension
(Matt 28:18-20; Mark 16:15-16; Luke 24:48; Acts 1:8). It is equally
clear that in the exercise of its ministry, the Church is commanded
to exercise the same ministry, as that of Jesus. That is to say, the
ministry of the Church cannot primarily be shaped or determined
by what the Church thinks or decides or yet by the needs of people
within or outside the Church, no matter how important those needs
are and no matter how important it is for those needs to be
addressed. Ministry can only rightly be shaped and determined by

the ministry of Jesus Christ. Any serious consideration of ministry must begin with consideration of Jesus Christ's ministry.

Ministry in the Church is first and foremost the ministry of the Triune God. Jesus - and he is God's minister *par excellence* - did not come introducing a new ministry of his own. He came manifesting and exercising God's ministry. As the Word of God made flesh, Jesus fulfilled and perfected God's purpose to redeem the world. Through his Word and Spirit, God had, in the course of their long history, revealed himself to Israel and called them into communion with himself. And in and through Israel, God called the world. Scripture reveals the glorious salvation that he offers an unworthy and sinful people and offers to an unworthy, sinful world. Jesus made that offer both possible and effectual. Through his substitutionary life, death, resurrection and ascension: he atoned for the sins of the world; conquered the powers of darkness and of hell which held men and women in their grip; rose victorious over all; and with love and power now offers to men and women deliverance from the power of sin. He offers to them his own righteous life, so that, clothed with that, they may be reconciled to the Father and become joint heirs with Christ in his kingdom. Jesus gathered up and fulfilled God's ministry of salvation.

The way in which God is portrayed and the way in which his ministry is fulfilled and demonstrated in Christ is all important. For the form and shape of God's ministry in Christ determines the form and shape of the Church's ministry.

The Scriptural Portrait

Scripture portrays God and his purpose to redeem the world in a most moving way. It portrays *God yearning over a world* that has sinned, refusing to cast it off, determined to redeem it and taking active measures for its salvation. It portrays God as holy, righteous and altogether loving. He hates and judges sin yet all the time loves his people and the world with an eternal love. In love he disciplines his people when they rebel against him, yet manifests towards them infinite patience when they sin. He is eternally merciful, unendingly forgiving and faithful.

Scripture renders this loving God in a variety of images. It portrays him as a *loving Father* who has called his people as a son out of Egypt. He carried them, 'as a father carries his son, all the way' through the wilderness until they reached the promised land (Deut 1:31).

It portrays him as a *loving Shepherd* who day and night watches over his people, guards them, protects them, blesses them and leads them to the pastures of the promised land. As a Shepherd, he provides for their needs and comfort, leads them gently along the right way, tenderly carrying in his arms the young and the weak. He matches each journey to their capabilities.

It portrays *God sorrowing over his people* in their sin, suffering along with them as they endure his disciplining of them, comforting them, telling them not to be afraid, for they are precious to him and he will go with them at all times, as they confront the trials of life.

Scripture portrays God as a *Husband to Israel* with whom he has made an everlasting covenant of marriage. Even when Israel behaves as an adulterous wife and goes after other lovers, worshipping other gods, God will not divorce her. He will not cast her off or abandon her. The people whom God primarily called were Israel. They exemplify all humankind and, in calling them, God was and is calling all people to share in his great salvation. In his loving embrace of them and his attitude to them we see his loving embrace and attitude to all the nations of the earth.

Jesus the Clearest Portrait

Jesus revealed in a clearer way all that had hitherto been revealed of God and his amazing love. He embodied and fulfilled God's purpose to redeem the world. He did so not only through what he said and taught, not only through what he did in works of compassion and healing, and not only through his atoning life, death, resurrection and ascension. He revealed God in and through his own *person*. For Jesus Christ was, and is, himself God, the Son of God. Jesus is 'the radiance of God's glory, and the exact representation of his being' (Heb 1:3, see Col 1:13). Jesus said, 'Anyone who has seen me, has seen the Father' and 'I and the Father are one' (John 14:9, 10:30).

Equally, he is one with the Father in the work of reconciliation. As Paul said, 'God was reconciling the world to himself in Christ' (2 Cor 5:19). Jesus said, 'I do what my Father does... the Father is in me, and I in the Father' (John 10:37-38).

As we cannot separate what Jesus said and did from his own person, so Jesus effected this work of reconciliation, not only by what he did in coming to earth, living, dying, rising again and ascending to the presence of the Father. He effected it in and through his own person. Coming on the side of God, and himself God, he represents God in his person to the people of the world. In Jesus we are confronted with all the fullness of God. Equally when Jesus took to himself human flesh and blood, he so identified himself with men and women that he became our representative. He represents, in his person, humanity to God. As God and as man, having atoned for the sins of the world, he reconciled God and humankind, uniting them in his own person.

The Ministry of Revelation and Reconciliation

Christ's ministry then is a ministry of revelation and of reconciliation through the Holy Spirit. Revelation and reconciliation are integral and central to his ministry. As such, they must be integral and central to the ministry of the Church.

Throughout his ministry, Christ always acted in love. Now we may not say as many people have tried to say that 'love is God'. This affirmation is not biblical and attempts to depersonalise God. We can and must say that 'God is love'. Love belongs to the mystery of God's personality. All that God does, he does in love. In his sovereign love, he made his covenant with Israel and with the world. In love he redeemed Israel, brought her into the promised land, watched over her, protected her and blessed her. When Israel sinned and rebelled against God, God judged and disciplined her but always in mercy and in love.

In the New Testament, God's love is poured out to the full in Jesus Christ. His love is expressed in the two words, *Jesus Christ*. Everything that Jesus said and did was with compassion and love. In compassion and love he taught and opened people's understanding to the things of God, addressed the needs of individuals, comforted the downcast and fallen, healed the sick, opened the eyes of the blind and the ears of the deaf, loosened the tongue of the dumb, cleansed the leper and raised the dead. He was and is the Good Shepherd.

The incarnation, death, resurrection and ascension of Jesus are proofs that God is love. 'This is how we know what love is: Jesus Christ laid down his life for us' (1 John 3:16). 'God demonstrates his own love for us in this: While we were still sinners, Christ died for us' (Rom 5:8, see John 3:16-17).

The Church's Ministry

The Church in her ministry is called to represent God in his ministry to the world, and to do so in a two-fold way. The Church is called to follow the pattern of Christ's ministry and to follow the example which he set. Jesus said, 'I have set you an example that you should do as I have done for you' (John 13:15). Paul said to the Christians in Corinth, 'Follow my example, as I follow the example of Christ' (1 Cor 11:1).

At the same time, the Church is called, through the Holy Spirit to share in Christ's own ministry, not in any ministry, not in a ministry of the Church's devising, but in Christ's ministry and thereby share in the ministry of the Triune God. There is no other ministry acceptable to God and able to advance his kingdom other than the ministry exercised by Jesus Christ. We share in that ministry by grace and through the Holy Spirit and the Word of God.

The Church is called so to open her life to God and surrender herself to God that when she lives and ministers God himself in Christ lives, speaks and ministers in and through her and manifests himself to the world. Through the Holy Spirit and the Word of God, the risen Christ, condescends to work out his own ministry within the Church and the Church shares in the ministry of Christ, and by grace becomes his instrument of revelation and reconciliation. In that context, Luke having written in his Gospel an account 'about all that Jesus began to do and teach until the day he was taken up to heaven' (Acts 1:1-2), wrote in the Acts of the Apostles about what the risen Christ continued to do by the power of the Holy Spirit in and through the life of the early Church. When anything is accomplished today for the furtherance of his kingdom, it is the risen Lord who accomplishes it in and through his Church. Christ is 'head over everything for the church, which is his body' (Eph 1:22-23).

If ever the Church in her ministry is not concerned to hold steadfastly to Christ through the Holy Spirit and the Word of God and to share in Christ's ministry of revelation and reconciliation, then the Church is out of step with God and is acting in disobedience to the Holy Spirit and the Word. The same is true of those who are called to minister within the Church. The Church of Christ is necessarily missionary and evangelistic.

Ministry belongs to the whole Church, not simply to those who are ordained to a particular ministry, within the Church. Jesus' commission to preach and make disciples and the promise of his presence was to all of his followers of every age. 'Go and make disciples of all nations, baptising them in the name of the Father and of the Son and of the Holy Spirit, and teaching them to obey everything I have commanded you. And surely I am with you always, to the very end of the age' (Matt 28:19-20).

It is unbiblical and detrimental to the life and work of the Church when this commission is interpreted as applying to other than to all believers. The Church is called and created to be a 'kingdom of priests' where everyone shares in the ministry of the Gospel that has been entrusted by Christ. When ministry is left to the few who are called to a particular ministry, then the Church loses much or most of its missionary vision and for the most part ceases to expand. This sadly is largely the case with the churches of the West today. It is of paramount importance for the whole Church to listen afresh to Christ's commission, to embrace that commission, to recover its evangelistic, missionary vision and become what God calls her to be, a 'kingdom of priests', and intercede for the world.

Because the early Church interpreted Christ's commission as applying to the whole Church so the Church grew and expanded rapidly. It was a missionary movement carried forward by the whole body of believers. When persecution broke out as it did, for example, when Stephen was martyred, the believers who fled the persecution took the good news of the Gospel with them wherever they went. They shared the Gospel with all who would hear and the Church continued to grow all the more. It was like someone endeavouring to put out a fire by scattering the ashes. Wherever the dispersed ashes fell, fresh fires broke out. This would seem to be how the Gospel first came to Rome, and the church in Rome was established, not through any particular leader of the Church but through ordinary believers fleeing the fires of persecution.

The Particular Office

Within the ministry committed to the whole Church, there is the call of some to the particular office of preaching, teaching, the administering of the sacraments and the pastoring of the people. They are called to exercise their ministry within the ministry of the whole Church and to help the whole Church to exercise her ministry. They do so at God's command. All ministry is his. He alone calls and commands men and women to serve him.

God's call can often startle the man or woman whom he confronts. They may rightly feel inadequate. Moses challenged by God before the burning bush pled his own weakness and inability, his lack of fluent speech. Jeremiah cried out, 'Ah, Sovereign Lord, I do not know how to speak; I am only a child' (Jer 1:6). Jesus said to his disciples, 'You did not choose me, but I chose you and appointed you to go and bear fruit - fruit that will last' (John 15:16).

The fact of God's call and command is a source of comfort and strength to all who are called to minister. I believe that there is no work which is more rewarding or fulfilling. Yet, it can be difficult, because we live in a sinful world and seek to minister to people who do not always wish to receive the Gospel. Because of the difficulties that confront us, it is a continuous source of strength and a necessary encouragement to any minister of the Gospel, that he or she did not choose the ministry (at least in the first instance). It was God who chose and called him or her. God's calling and commands undergird their ministry and give it strength and courage and joy in times of adversity.

At the same time, because all of us are sinful and tempted to sloth, the awareness of God's command and the fact that we must give account to him, help to keep us faithful and diligent in our calling.

I believe that there is no more satisfying part of the ministry and no part which is spiritually more uplifting and strengthening to the minister's own faith, than the pastoral. To engage with people, to see God working in another person's life, to see someone grow spiritually or come to a living saving faith in Christ, for the first time, is immensely uplifting and satisfying for the minister, especially if the minister has had, under God, some small part in that. The pastoral ministry brings a minister and congregation very close together. Yet pastoral work and visitation is tiring. Often a minister, out of physical weariness, or reasons of other work and pressures, can be tempted to neglect the pastoral side of the ministry and pastoral visitation. This is sad and can lead to the spiritual impoverishment both of the minister and the congregation.

Love

Because the Church is called to represent God in his ministry to the world, so the church must always act in love. The Church can only represent God and reflect and share in Christ's ministry when the Church acts in the same love and manifests the same understanding and tender compassion that Christ does to everyone. Nothing so mars the ministry of the Church and hinders the work of the Holy Spirit more than quarrelling and division within the Church. The Holy Spirit is the Spirit of love and unity and only works where there is love and unity in Christ.

This is a tremendous challenge to all in the Church and to every minister. Without love we cannot fulfil the calling of the ministry: we cannot faithfully represent Christ in his holiness and love to our people or to the world. It is so easy to become impatient and act and speak without love. Moses and Aaron misrepresented the holiness, love and patience of God in the face of Israel's sin at Meribah. As a result they were not allowed to enter the promised land. The Lord said to Moses, 'You too will be gathered to your people, as your brother Aaron was, for when the community rebelled at the waters in the Desert of Zin, both of you disobeyed my command to honour me as holy before their eyes' (Num 27:13-14, see Deut 32:50-52).

How often have we sinned, as Moses and Aaron sinned, in misrepresenting God in Christ? Try as we might, we are not able of ourselves to produce the love which alone can sustain, enthuse and fulfil our ministry. For love is a gift from God. We need to ask for it in prayer, not once nor twice, but every day. I believe as ministers that there are certain things we need to pray for every day. We need every day to ask for God to give us the gift of love, and to give it in ever greater measure, so that we may love as Christ does, love our families, our congregations and everyone without exception. It was said by a Roman governor writing to his superiors in Rome, 'How these Christians love one another!'. Would that that could be said of the Church today and said of each of our ministries!

As revelation and reconciliation were the centre of God's ministry in Christ, and must be the centre of the Church's ministry, so also these must be at the centre of the preaching and the pastoral ministry of the Church. 'All this is from God, who reconciled us to himself through Christ and gave us the ministry of reconciliation: that God was reconciling the world to himself in Christ, not counting men's sins against them. And he has committed to us the message of reconciliation' (2 Cor 5:18-19).

Making God Known

We are called to make God known in the whole way that he revealed himself to Israel and the world and revealed himself in Christ. We are called to make him known as a God of holiness and righteousness, as a God of mercy and of love who has worked out a great salvation and offers that salvation freely to all who will receive him and his love and salvation.

We are called to make God known in his Person as Redeemer in Christ. To know God in that way, is not simply to know what God said or taught or did. All that is very important. For there can be no true understanding of God apart from what he said and did in Christ and through history. To know God in his Person as Redeemer is to know him in his Triune nature of Father, Son and Holy Spirit. To know him in that way is life itself, life eternal.

The emphasis on the Personhood of God in his Triune nature, as a God who saves, has far reaching implications for ministry. For, in our preaching and pastoral ministry our aim is not primarily to speak about God. It is not primarily to tell people what to do (and as ministers we can be too ready to do that!). Our primary task is to present the Triune Person of God as Father, Son and Holy Spirit. We want people to meet God face to face in Jesus Christ. We want them through the Holy Spirit to see his glory, his radiance, his love, to receive his forgiveness, to experience his deliverance and to enter into fellowship with him.

In preaching and in pastoral ministry we dare not direct attention to ourselves, to our preaching or our oratory. If we do this, we will turn people's attention away from Christ and will hinder the work of the Gospel. Our aim must always be to direct attention to God in his Triune nature. John the Baptist said, 'He must become greater; I must become less' (John 3:30). Our constant prayer must ever be that in preaching and through worship, as in pastoral care, people will become deeply aware of God's presence and will hear him speaking to them in love and saving power. We want people to meet personally with God in Christ Jesus. We are called in the words of Paul in Gal 3:27 to be 'clothed with Christ'.

Because our one desire is that people meet with God in Christ, so we must ever seek to draw alongside of people where they are. We must seek in love to understand them, if possible, to think as they think, to look out on the world as they do. This involves our loving them in Christ, our listening to them as they share their understanding and their experience of people and of things. It involves our listening to their understanding of God. It calls from our part continued prayer, a readiness to stand back, as occasion demands, and an understanding of when to stand back, in order that our people might be alone with God. This is not easy, but we learn and grow with our people as we keep close to Christ in prayer and are sensitive to their needs. Our one desire is that they meet God for themselves in Jesus Christ.

The Ministry of Prayer

Jesus' ministry was a ministry of prayer. He prayed constantly. He prayed all night before he chose the twelve apostles (Luke 6:12-13). He prayed for them in the hour of trial (Mark 6:46-48). He prayed for Simon Peter that his 'faith may not fail' (Luke 22:31-32). He prayed for those who crucified him (Luke 23:34). He always lives to pray for us' (Rom 8:34; Heb 7:25; 1 John 2:1).

To share through the Spirit in the ministry of Christ Jesus involves on our part a life of prayer and communion with Christ. Only Christ can change people and give them a new understanding and create within them a hunger and a love for God and give us the grace helpfully to minister to them. We are utterly dependent all the time on Christ to work effectively through our ministry.

When we do not pray we are not following the example of Jesus nor sharing in his ministry and our people suffer. Our ministry ceases to be effective. People may be drawn to us or to the Church but they are not drawn to the Lord. Lives are not changed. In parish visiting, I have found great value in praying however briefly before knocking on each door and before each pastoral encounter.

Our aim, like Paul's, is that before the eyes of our people Jesus Christ crucified and risen be 'clearly portrayed' (Gal 3:1). Professor Karl Barth used to say to his students, 'I know no God but the man Christ Jesus'. In the man Jesus, we come face to face with God himself, in all his fullness, and power to save. In Jesus, we meet God as Saviour. Therefore in all our ministry, we are seeking to help people to be aware of Jesus Christ, to meet him and know him, whom to know is life eternal.

In every Church Membership Class, I have tried to stress the centrality of Jesus Christ in our understanding of God. I have endeavoured to stress that whenever we meet together to worship God and whenever we pray, publicly or privately, we should seek to be aware that the Jesus of the Gospel story is truly present in the midst and speaking to us. For, when he is present all that is of God is present. Jesus is taking our worship and our prayers, cleansing them, sanctifying them and uniting them with his own as he presents them to the Father. In this way our worship is accepted, our prayers are heard and answered.

Salvation By Grace

The Gospel to which we bear testimony is a Gospel of grace. Salvation is a gift of grace. To the natural man it is hard to realise or accept that salvation is not something which we can achieve or earn as a reward. It is a gift of God's grace which we receive as we receive Christ. It cannot be detached from the Person of Christ. This must ever be before us in our preaching and pastoral work.

In receiving salvation as a gift of God's grace we become completely changed. Unless we become changed in the process we do not and cannot receive God's salvation. A true understanding of God is never simply intellectual. True knowledge of God is practical, involving prayer and obedience. We know him only as we open our lives to him and seek in our understanding of him to become like Jesus Christ and to be united to him in Jesus Christ. Such understanding involves humility, listening, obedience, and the surrender of ourselves to God. It involves the whole of us. As Jesus said (John 7:17), 'If anyone chooses to do God's will, he will find out whether my teaching comes from God'. Only when we obey him, and as we become conformed to Christ, do we understand Christ.

True preaching therefore must be theological in that it presents God in his love and determination to save the world. It must also be practical and evangelical in that it summons people to respond in obedience, to accept Christ, to be conformed to Christ, to obey and serve him. The same emphasis applies to our pastoral work as we keep before us the content and nature of the Gospel that we seek to make known.

As prayer is important so our people must be encouraged to pray and taught how to pray in the name of Jesus, so that they may not only hear but receive the Gospel and enter into the joy of Christ's salvation. Sadly today many people never pray and many do not know how to pray. In this situation, preaching about prayer from the pulpit is generally not enough and hearing the minister pray in the pulpit is not enough. To teach them, as ministers we must be ready personally to pray with them where they are, voicing with them, on their behalf, their needs before God and the needs of their loved ones and friends. It is difficult to know how otherwise they will learn to pray unless we in our pastoral work actually pray for them and with them. As they hear us pray with them where they are, voicing their needs, they learn by grace to pray.

The Ministry of Reconciliation

The concern for reconciliation must influence our preaching. Like Peter on the day of Pentecost we must be ever ready to call on people to repent, to receive Christ as Saviour and to be baptised. Peter's sermons give us a pattern to follow in our preaching.

Likewise the concern for reconciliation with God must guide all our pastoral work. In visiting, in talking, in praying with our people our deep prayerful concern must be that they are reconciled to God and in reconciliation grow in grace and obedience and faith. So often our congregational visitation can become simply routine. It can become purely social visitation, where we come in a social way to know and befriend our people. Social visitation and friendship with our people is important and essential for effective ministry. If our visitation however is no more than that, if we fail to lift the eyes and hearts of our people to Christ and fail to try and help them into a living saving relationship with God or help them to grow in that relationship, then we are failing in our ministry. We are not being true shepherds of the flock. We are in danger of becoming what the Bible calls 'false shepherds or hirelings' who are content to leave the sheep to their fate, without the salvation of God. Scripture has much to say about false shepherds of the flock.

Today, there is great emphasis on counselling. There are counselling courses in our universities where people are trained to be professional counsellors. Counselling today is recommended and offered in almost every situation of life. There is great value in this. We can be grateful for all the new insights and skills acquired through counselling and for all that is being offered to people in need. There is considerable difference however between the work of a counsellor and that of a pastor, who is seeking by the grace of God to share in Christ's ministry to his people. We must not confuse the two. If our work as ministers does not go beyond that of counselling, if in our pastoral work we are not seeking prayerfully to help people to personal faith in Jesus Christ, to the enjoyment of his salvation and to Christian service, then, we might be good counsellors in the accepted sense today, but we are failing in our ministry. Christ's ministry is our pattern and the only ministry that can build or extend the Kingdom of God. We are called as pastors to share in his ministry and in his Name to call people into reconciliation with God. This cannot be emphasised enough.

Occasions for Ministry

Certain occasions offer great opportunity in ministry. As Christ operates in a wonderful way through the sacraments of baptism and holy communion, so the preparation of our people for these sacraments present some of the most effective ways of building Christ's Church. Parents are deeply moved through the birth of a child and frequently wide open to receive the Gospel. The teaching of parents the meaning of baptism and of the grace of God that is offered to their children, the teaching of parents about the need to pray with their children from their birth, the encouragement to face up to their God-given parental responsibilities, can help many to come more fully into the fold of the Church. The teaching about holy communion, the preparation of people for their first celebration, offers unparalleled opportunities for the building up of people's faith and the extension of the Church.

Likewise, occasions of marriage, sickness, accident, death and bereavement bring a minister very close to his or her people. People respond to understanding, kindness and compassion and often are ready to listen to and receive the Gospel in a way in which they often are not open in other periods of their lives. At these turning points in their lives many can be led to faith in Christ. The minister must ever 'Preach the Word; be prepared in season and out of season... with great patience and careful instruction' (2 Tim 4:2)

Prayers for Pastors

As one who for many years has tried to be a pastor to my people as well as a preacher of the Gospel, I offer out of my own experience the following suggestions:

• *Pray every day for the gift of love.* Pray that Christ's love may be given to you in ever greater measure, so that you will love your congregation as Christ loves them. Pray that you will love everyone and love your partner in marriage and your family (if this applies). None of us can love as Jesus loves. We need constantly, daily, to

pray for this gift in ever greater measure. It comes as a lovely surprise
that after a while we become aware that God is graciously answering
our prayers and giving us his gift of love.

Being human, we may at times differ from our office-bearers
in our understanding of the Church and its work or we may in the
congregation experience with someone a clash of personality. How
important to pray that we will love each one in Christ. Love brings
peace and joy into our lives and the lives of others. It creates the
environment in which alone the Holy Spirit can work.

• *Pray to be conformed to the likeness of Christ.* It was said of John
Livingstone, the minister, who was mightily used of God in the
Shotts revival in 1630, that he felt it was far more important for
him to be in prayer and to allow God to put his life right with God
than to spend time in sermon preparation. For most ministers, it
may be a dangerous principle not to spend considerable time in
sermon preparation. When our lives, however, are in tune with
God and we are in harmony with Christ, undoubtedly our
ministries are more effective. Livingstone's ministry testified to the
truth of this and it is something to which many of us would testify.

• *Pray to be filled with the Holy Spirit.* The risen Lord in
commissioning his disciples to go forth and witness to him, 'in
Jerusalem, and in all Judea and Samaria, and to the ends of the
earth', told them first to wait until the 'the Holy Spirit comes on
you' (Acts 1:8). For then they would receive power and would
witness effectively. We need every day to pray, as ministers, and
ask that we will be filled afresh with God's Holy Spirit of power
and love and with Christ's victory over the world.

• *Pray to be a good listener.* People need someone to talk to, someone
who will listen, who will begin to understand their problems and
concerns and be sympathetic. Everyone needs and wants that. As
Christians we are called to listen to the world's problems, to understand
the needs of other people so that we can help them to find the
answer to their needs in Christ. Of ourselves we may have no answer
to give. Christ has the answer to all our problems. People need the
Church and need us as ministers lovingly, sympathetically to
accompany them into the presence of Christ so that they may lay
all their problems at the feet of him who said, 'Come to me, all you
who are weary and burdened, and I will give you rest' (Matt 11:28).

- *Pray for wisdom and practical insight* in order to know what to say and do in every situation. In Paul's prayers for the younger churches when he himself was in prison, he prayed that they might grow continually in their knowledge and love of God. But he also prayed that they might have practical wisdom and know what they ought to do in their daily lives. As Christians we constantly need this practical wisdom as we engage in the life and work of the Church. We need to know what to say and when to say it in our pastoral conversations. We need a wisdom that is not naturally ours and which is not of this world. It is a wisdom that God has promised to give to all who ask in faith (James 1:5). If only we as ministers were more diligent in asking for the wisdom of God how different our ministries would be!

- *Pray for courage* always to say what is right and helpful, always to witness to Christ. Peter and John were arrested and brought before the Sanhedrin. They were commanded with threats 'not to speak or teach at all in the name of Jesus' (Acts 4:18). On their release, however, they did not pray that they would be spared from further persecution. They prayed for courage faithfully to proclaim Christ, even in the face of persecution (Acts 4:29). How often we in the ministry and as Christians have missed valuable God-given opportunities to witness to Christ and to say what God is wanting us to say, all because of fear of what others would think. We have lacked boldness in Christ.

- *Pray that God will graciously work his miracles of grace* in Christ and that God will break down the barriers of sin and unbelief, which keep people from him and from the enjoyment of his salvation. Only Christ can open eyes that are blind and make cold hearts receptive to the Gospel. We need to know and believe that God wants to do that and will do that when the Church is faithful and as the Church prays. When Jesus returned to his home town of Nazareth, we read that, 'He did not do many miracles there because of their lack of faith' (Matt 13:58). Sadly, it often seems today that God does no mighty work because of our unbelief. We need to *pray for faith* that God will work miracles today in our generation and through our ministries. The whole of the Christian faith is miraculous. It could not be otherwise when God is unseen and known only through faith. We should therefore expect miracles and pray for miracles.

Pastoral Questions to Ask

There are however a number of questions which we can ask, very gently, in our pastoral work. These are questions which I have used regularly and found helpful in my ministry. I have not found that people have minded or taken offence at my asking them. Frequently, I have found a measure of relief on their part and gratitude that I have asked them.

'Do you pray?' Many people today do not pray or find difficulty in praying. Unless we know their difficulties and where they stand spiritually, it is difficult for us to help them. When they do find praying difficult it is right that we give them in a clear and simple way all the help that we can. Passages of Scripture which are prayers, particularly the Psalms, are helpful and also many hymns. We can ask them to read the suggested passage or hymn and make it their prayer. Sometimes it is enough to guide a person what to pray and leave them to pray to God on their own. Sometimes, people need more practical help and need the minister to pray along with them and, often, to pray sentence by sentence after the minister, before they can go forward and pray on their own. In my experience, professional people, possibly because of a greater tendency to unbelief, have often required on their first occasion, to pray sentence by sentence after me. Thereafter, they were able to continue on their own. I have found less educated people often more able than professional people to do this on their first occasion of prayer.

I have found it very valuable as a pastor, when visiting in home or hospital, on every occasion that is possible, to pray with my people. If we ask to commit the person's circumstances to God and ask God's blessings on that person and on his or her family, in my experience of over forty years in the ministry, it is rare, even among non-church members for prayer not to be welcomed. In hospital, in the face of illness or before an operation, it is especially welcomed.

If we do not pray in the home or in hospital, with our people, then we are not providing the spiritual help and encouragement that we should. It is also more difficult to teach them how to pray in a practical way.

If I have asked regularly, "Do you pray?" I may add, *'What do you say in prayer?'* For example, Do you give thanks?' Thanksgiving is so important in the Christian life. Faith is primarily thanksgiving for the great things that God has done for us in Christ, is doing today and will yet do. Unless we give thanks and teach our people to give thanks at all times, then our and their faith will not grow as it ought; and we will not discern as we ought the love of God.

In regard to prayer, I always ask, *'Do you ask God for forgiveness?* Do you find this difficult? Do you do it regularly? Can you forgive others? Can you ask other people for their forgiveness? Can you forgive yourself?'* Whereas I am not aware that anyone has ever minded my asking whether they pray (and in over forty years I have asked hundreds of people that question), it is different when the question of forgiveness is raised. I have found in asking this question that the atmosphere can change instantly and dramatically. In my experience approximately one person in twenty can express anger, not I believe against the minister but against God or other people. The anger results from sin that has never been confessed and from hurt that has been repressed.

In these situations, I have always asked, *'What is the problem?'*. At that point, the pastoral visit really begins as lovingly and tenderly I have tried as a pastor to direct that person to the love and forgiveness of God in Christ. I have endeavoured to direct his or her mind to various passages of Scripture which might seem appropriate. As a prayer for forgiveness, I have frequently invited a person to read Psalm 51 and make it their prayer to God. There are few passages of Scripture which are more powerful and helpful to someone in need of forgiveness. I have seen lives completely changed, people converted, through using this Psalm as a prayer.

I have asked, *'Do you pray for others?* Can you say that you pray for others more than you pray for yourself?'*. It is a great test of our Christian character that we pray more for other people and pray for Christ's world-wide Kingdom.

It is also important to ask, *'Do you read the Bible?* Do you find it difficult to read and understand?'* It is important that people discover that the Bible is the place of encounter between God and his people and if they read it in the right way with prayer they will meet with God and hear him speaking to them in Christ. We need to give considerable practical help to people to enable them to do this helpfully.

I have long felt that as a minister it is one of my prime responsibilities to teach and encourage people to pray and to read God's Word. If they do read and meditate day by day on God's

Word they will grow steadily in Christ and through the Holy Spirit they will learn far more than ever I can teach them.

Likewise I have asked, *'Do you worship regularly in Church?* Are you aware of God's love?" "Are you aware of God calling you to serve him?'. The answers to these questions lead on to further pastoral conversation and further suggested help can be given.

In pastoral conversation, as a minister, I have frequently found that whereas a person may have faith in God, nonetheless there seems to be something which is holding that person back from further growth in the Lord. Often in these situations, I have asked, *'Have you had a happy childhood?'*. I have found that there are few more valuable questions to ask than this one. I have never found a person taking offence at my asking it. Often I have been deeply disturbed by the answers that I have received. When we ourselves have had a happy childhood we tend to assume that everyone else in the Church, or even in society, has had a happy childhood. How wrong we are to think that! Many people have encountered very sad situations in childhood. Think of the number of broken marriages and what that has meant to countless numbers of children and we begin to understand. More than we like to think, have been abused and many have been sexually abused. People nurse hurts that go back into the early years of childhood. Many nurse grievances and have never been able to forgive those who have wronged them. Until these hurts are given over to God and a person learns to forgive they will not enjoy the peace of God or experience the joy of his forgiveness for their sins. The question, 'Have you had a happy childhood?', put tenderly and lovingly, can open the way for considerable pastoral help to be given and healing to be received.

The Apostle Paul embodied in a remarkable way the ministry of Christ and has set a challenging example to all who are called to the preaching and pastoral ministry. Would that all of us could say what he could say about his ministry! I conclude with words taken from his first Epistle to the Thessalonians. 'You are witnesses, and so is God, of how holy, righteous and blameless we were among you who believed. For you know that we dealt with each of you as a father deals with his own children, encouraging, comforting and urging you to live lives worthy of God, who calls you into his kingdom and glory' (1 Thess 2:10-12).

Stoking the Fire

1 What is the connection between the ministry of Jesus and the ministry given to the church?

2 Of what importance is the pastoral side of ministry? What happens when we neglect pastoral ministry? When we tend to it?

3 What happens in our ministry when we pray with and for people? What happens when we neglect such prayer?

4 How is true preaching to be both theological and practical?

5 Which questions about prayer would you be willing to ask someone?

6 Which of Torrance's 'pastoral questions' would you like to ask in your congregation and why?

Ignition Points

Husband and wife in their relationship are called to reflect the infinite patience, compassion, forgiveness and love which God always shows in his covenant relationship with us and his people.

When each gives thanks to God for the other, then marriage has a new dimension, with the partner as God's gift. This gives to marriage a deep sense of sanctity and permanency. To opt out of it would be tantamount to turning one's back on God.

The Gospel proclaims that God has not abandoned man and woman in their most intimate relationship. In Christ, God goes with them. He is present in Christian marriage, continually creating it and building it to his glory and our mutual comfort and happiness.

Jesus Christ commands that we love and cherish one another as he loves and cherishes us even unto death.

The man become truly man in relation to the woman and the woman becomes truly woman in the relation to the man. This in no way denies that a single man or woman can by the grace of God find complete fulfilment in Christ.

Because of our inability always to maintain the sanctity and permanence of the marriage bond, the Bible in its teaching accepts divorce, when we are faced with the irretrievable breakdown in marriage. This does not mean the hallowing of divorce... both parties need the cleansing and forgiveness of God.

Where one or both have previously been divorced, I always ask them to have a time alone with God in prayer. I ask them to commit to God the whole of their past and to ask and receive God's forgiveness for all that needs to be forgiven and to set them free.

Chapter Six

MARRIAGE IN THE COVENANT OF CHRIST

David W. Torrance

Christ has laid hold of our broken, sinful humanity and restored it with his own perfect humanity. He has offered as a human being the response to God we could never offer on our own. Now he does not remain aloof from us nor from our most intimate relationships. Rather, he is the third person in every Christian marriage, the one in whom the union between husband and wife occurs. In this way, Christian marriage testifies to the world the grace found in Christ Jesus. It signifies the mystery of the union between Christ and his bride, the church. David Torrance examines in this chapter how marriage is both a gift and a calling from God, and how every Christian marriage is ultimately grounded in Christ.

In seeking a Biblical doctrine of marriage, we should consider not only individual texts, but the whole meaning of Scripture and how it points to an understanding of God which in turn sheds light on our life together in marriage. When interpreted in this light, the Bible has much to say about marriage and not, as some today affirm, very little.

The Reformers held that, whereas marriage is created and ordained by God for everyone in the world, in Christ God has sanctified and redeemed marriage from its state in the fallen world and restored it to its original character and purpose as taught by Jesus himself (Matt 19:4-6). In its deepest sense true marriage, Christian marriage, is altogether different from an unchristian marriage. It is of a different order, for, it is 'in Christ'.

Marriage may not be broken. If it is, not only is the relationship of man and woman scarred, but the relationship of each with God is also marred. Adultery is an attack on God, not simply on a partner (Psalm 51:4).

In the Old Testament, marriage is called to mirror the relationship of love and grace which God chose to enter into with his people Israel. Israel is called God's spouse (see Hosea). In the New Testament it mirrors the relationship of Jesus Christ with all his beloved followers, and the Church is called the bride of the Lamb (Eph 5:25-32, Rev 21:2). This is the wonderful relationship into which we are called by God in Christ. Husband and wife in their relationship one with another in marriage are called to reflect the infinite patience, endurance, compassion, forgiveness and love which God continually shows in his covenant relationship with us and his people. Jesus said, 'As the Father has loved me, so have I loved you. Now remain in my love... Love each other as I have loved you' (John 15:9,12).

CHRISTIAN MARRIAGE AND COVENANT

In marriage, we are called to reflect Christ and the grace and beauty of his covenant relationship with his people. Through his Holy Spirit it is grounded on and sealed by and within his covenant.

The Reformers viewed the event of marriage in a way not unlike that in which believing Jews continue, from Old Testament times, to understand it as involving a relationship with God within the sacred bond of the covenant. According to Old Testament Scripture, Jews may not marry someone outside the covenant, that is, someone who does not believe in the Living God and who has not identified himself or herself with the covenant people (Deut 7:3-4 etc). According to the Talmud, whereas there is a form of marriage for the Gentile world that is of God, marriage in its deepest sense before God only takes place within the covenant and 'in the Name of Heaven'. Therefore, to 'marry out', is for orthodox Jews a very serious matter. It is held to involve a denial of one's faith. The one who does it cuts himself or herself off from the believing community, and from the parent family. For devout Jews the words of Hosea 2:19,20 form an integral part of the marriage service. These are the words which God speaks in renewing his covenant with Israel. Standing with his bride within the canopy, or *chuppa*, the bridegroom affirms these words of God's covenant and affirms them with regard to his bride thereby affirming that his marriage is embraced or inter-locked within the covenant. 'I will betroth you to me for ever; I will betroth you in righteousness and justice, in love and compassion. I will betroth you in faithfulness, and you will acknowledge the Lord.' Thereupon the bride and bridegroom are handed a cup of wine, the wine being a sacrament or seal of their union. It is their belief, that without wine the marriage would not be sealed, that is, no wine no wedding, which helps us to understand the significance of the miracle in Cana of Galilee, when Jesus turned water into wine, presumably to allow the wedding to proceed. In the New Testament, Paul, deeply influenced by the Old Testament and by Rabbinic teaching, affirms that a Christian must always marry a Christian (2 Cor 6:14); marriage is 'in the Lord'; there, by grace, it reflects God's relationship with his people, and is sealed by the body and blood of Christ.

The considerable loss of the Jewish roots of our faith and the failure to take the Old Testament seriously has prevented many Christians from understanding the significance and depth of the biblical teaching on marriage. In Christ God has set our life on the new basis of his grace in which he gives himself wholly, unreservedly, to us in redeeming love and calls forth from us a corresponding movement of love and self-giving in Christ. We are summoned through his love to give ourselves in love to one another in Christ. We are to love one another in the same way and to the same extent in Christ as he loves us. Within that context, husband and wife are called in marriage to give themselves unreservedly, totally, one to the other in the Lord, such that they interlock and become one flesh, and in a sense one whole person. As one whole person they are called in their intimate personal relationships with one another to reflect God in his relationships with us. Marriage in Christ, Christian marriage, is drawn into the covenant relations of God with his people. It is grounded on it, and God's covenant gives it shape.

The Biblical teaching on marriage has a number of practical implications:

1   Marriage is a gift and call from God

It is sacred, and very precious. It evokes a sense of wonder and thanks to God. When each gives thanks to God for the other, then marriage has a new dimension - the partner is God's special gift. This gives to marriage a deep sense of sanctity and permanency. To opt out of it would be tantamount to turning one's back on God.

God calls a particular man and woman into a life partnership. His calling embraces the whole area of both their lives and lasts, not for a temporary period, but as long as they live. No third person can share that calling - not even their own child. They enter into it in their freedom and through their love for each other. When we recognise marriage both as a calling of God and as God's gift, then it acquires its true dignity - 'for better or for worse; for richer, for poorer; in sickness and in health; to love and to cherish' each other until death parts them.

2   Marriage is about faithfulness, and hard work

In giving us marriage, God calls us into life-partnership. To this extent marriage is more than ordinary human endeavour. Marriage must spring from love if it is to take shape as a life partnership. It must continually be fed and sustained by love if it is to grow and blossom and bring joy to the participants.

In this respect the relationship of two people in marriage is somewhat akin to Israel's relationship with God. God called Israel into lasting covenant relationship. God remained faithful in his calling and in his love for his people. But through the long years of the Old Testament era, his people were frequently wayward, unfaithful, unloving and unhappy. It took long years of personal encounter and partnership with the living God, years of hardship and suffering, years of striving after God in obedience and faith and love, before Israel, as represented by the Apostles and the believers, became the people who really rejoiced in their covenant partnership.

A happy life partnership does not just come about once a man and a woman have been married. It does not automatically arise, even when a man and woman genuinely love one another. It is something which must be sought after and worked for and prayed for.

3   Marriage is part of creation, and so God sustains it

Marriage is not just a human, social institution as so many wish to affirm today. It is affirmed as God's act (Gen 2:18-25) and re-affirmed by Jesus (Matt 19:4-6, Mark 10:6-9). All the Churches affirm this Scriptural position. In this secular age in which we live, when many couples choose to live together without wishing to get married, the Church must proclaim and insist that marriage is of God. It belongs to his act of creation and to his purpose for humankind and was taken up and affirmed in his act of redemption.

Yet God did not simply create marriage back in the beginning, and then, as it were, leave man and woman in their freedom to get on with their relationship with each other and to work out their marriage in their own way, as best they might. Thankfully he does not so leave any individual man or woman who trusts him and whom he has called into marriage. Left to themselves each partner in a marriage could and frequently would seek to struggle in their sin for a false individualism, to assert himself or herself and to dominate or tyrannise over the other.

The Gospel proclaims that God has not abandoned man and woman in their most intimate relationship. In Christ God goes with a Christian man and woman. He is present in Christian marriage continually creating and building it to his glory and to man's and woman's mutual comfort and happiness. By his Holy Spirit he brings us again and again to the cross in humility, repentance and renewal. For the cross is the place where we are made by the Holy Spirit to die to ourselves and to rise ever again as a new person, one new person, man and wife, in Christ Jesus. This is something which must and does happen again and again. Having committed ourselves, our love and our marriage to the Lord, the Lord presides over our marriage, he assumes the responsibility for deepening our love and building our marriage, seeking to perfect it through the years. In Christian marriage, God is always present in all his creative redeeming power and love.

4   Marriage is a total fellowship of love, for life

In his covenant with us in Christ, God gave himself to us, and goes on giving himself to us, in all his wholeness and entirety. This is the incredible wonder and mystery of the Incarnation - something happened to God! God has given himself and goes on giving himself in entirety to us in Christ. In Christ he has for ever united men and women to himself. And as his giving to us is total, so his claim on us is total. He claims that we give our all to him, and in doing this, so also we give our all one to another. We may not give only part of ourselves to the other and be blessed by him. We cannot rightly be married to our partner and at the same time be married, for example, to our work or pleasure, far less to someone else. We can no longer see, hear, think, speak or live apart from that other who is our partner in marriage. Of course, we are all sinful and sadly in our individualism and self-centredness, we fall short of God's ideal.

This, however, is what God calls us to do and what each couple must strive to do in Christ. It is what is involved in 'becoming one flesh', that is 'one whole person'.

The totality of that physical-spiritual loving and caring to which a man and woman are called in marriage is only possible in a monogamous relationship where all others are excluded. Marriage portrays God's covenant relationship with us. In Scripture God is portrayed as jealous of any other would-be lover to whom we might give our affection. He is single and wholehearted in his love for us and demands of us a single and wholehearted love for him. Our love for him must, as it were, be monogamous and in our oneness with him in the Spirit he demands that our love for one another as husband and wife be monogamous.

Clearly, God's people took a long time to understand and accept that monogamy is God's will. In the Old Testament, polygamy was widely practised even by the fathers in the faith quite unthinkingly (despite Gen 2:18-25, the Song of Songs, Hosea and Mal 2:13-16). But when we turn to the New Testament and to the coming of Christ as the fulfilment of the covenant, polygamy immediately disappears. Never did the Church doubt this or hesitate over it. The Apostles and early Church clearly understood the covenant and its fulfilment in Christ Jesus as the true basis of monogamy. It is probable, as this writer believes, that their certainty about the rightness of monogamy follows on from the miracle at the marriage in Cana in Galilee. Following that marriage, which took place in a Jewish context, Jesus Christ was seen henceforth as the Lord over marriage, the One in and through whom alone the marriage between one man and woman takes place. The Apostle said, 'He revealed his glory' (John 2:11).

This is all the more significant when we consider that the Jews who did not accept Jesus Christ continued to practice polygamy. Many of them continued to do so right up to the thirteenth and fourteenth centuries and only embraced monogamy when compelled to do so by the laws of the country in which they resided. Equally significant is the fact that no other religion in the world, other than the Christian religion, has of its own accord embraced monogamy or given to men and women that mutual dignity and status which is demanded in a true monogamous relationship.

5 Our physical sexuality is of God

Since God claims the whole person, and requires that in marriage man and woman give themselves totally to one another, so his claim and demand sanctifies our physical sexuality. God has created our physical as well as our spiritual being and so sanctifies both. Hence, the sexual desires of husband and wife for each other are in themselves good, holy and lovely. They are an integral part of their whole being in relationship to God and each other. God in creating and sanctifying man, male and female, includes their sexuality within their humanity, so that the physical love with which they love one another is important, integral to their whole love for one another.

Any feeling of guilt or shame in this sphere is misplaced. Instead there is great cause for joy and thanksgiving. As our physical nature is a vital part of our being, so our physical nature and sexuality are a vital, God-given part of our relationship in marriage. The words, 'they will become one flesh' (Gen 2:24, cf. 1 Cor 6:16) undoubtedly refers to physical, sexual, as well as spiritual union. Sexual desires and true love are indissolubly united in marriage. Marriage is a question of the whole man and the whole woman and of the total union of both.

6 Trial marriages, and sex outside of marriage

Because God's claim on us is all-embracing, there is no room in Christian thinking for trial marriages, where there is no total commitment to the other for life. Likewise, there can be no exploring or expressing our sexuality before entering total commitment in marriage.

Again, there must be no extra-marital sexual relationships. Various passages of Scripture expressly forbid each and all of these. The whole thrust of Scripture, the placing of Christian marriage within the covenant which was renewed and sealed in Jesus Christ, through his atoning sacrifice, make these kind of sexual relationships incompatible with our union in Christ. This goes far deeper than simply offending against certain biblical texts.

In sum, true marriage is patterned on and reflects God's covenant relationship with us. It takes place within the covenant, is grounded in, conditioned and sealed by that covenant and demands that a man and a woman give themselves totally in love for life to God and to each other.

Jesus Christ commands that we love and cherish one another as he loves and cherishes us even to the death. None of us in our sin and individualism is able fully to do that. Therefore all of us need, day by day, to kneel before the cross that we might continually share in Christ's death and resurrection. As we die with Christ to our sin and our sinful selves so we rise united with each other in Christ. For a happy, fulfilled marriage, we need to pray day by day that Jesus Christ will live in us and we in him, clothed together with his righteousness, purity and love.

SOME RELATED ISSUES

1   Men and women in relationship

This has been an area of great controversy, and, sadly, considerable oppression - usually of women by men (though today it is recognised that the reverse also happens). Whereas in early times the Christian faith was a liberator of women, in later years it has been used to justify holding women down - usually because of considering specific texts without understanding the whole scope of the Bible.

God calls men and women in marriage into relationship with each other. They are equal in dignity and status before God, they are equally loved by God and are called to share equally in his glory and divine inheritance. At the same time they are different, and are given a different responsibility and are called to a different service - so, they are able to help one another and each to complement the other's need in accord with the purpose of God (Gen 1:27f.). In marriage, for mutual happiness it is important that each acknowledges that the other is of equal importance to God and equally loved by God. The one must not seek to dominate the other or seek to deny to the other his or her rightful contribution and service. Each must rejoice in his or her own manhood or womanhood and rejoice in that of the partner.

The man becomes truly man in relation to the woman and the woman becomes truly woman in relation to the man. This in no way denies that a single man or woman can by the grace of God find complete fulfilment in Christ. We must affirm that they can and do. Yet in the order of God's creation and in the creation of marriage, each finds his or her fulfilment in and through the other. In genuine love and care each must encourage the other to be what they are and without in the least feeling threatened by the other's sexuality encourage and assist the other to make their maximum contribution. In encouraging and enjoying the fulfilment of the other in their sexuality, the partner is also fulfilled.

2 Men and Women in a Wider Context

The difference between men and women is not limited to the biological sphere in that women have children and men do not. The difference of men and women affects their entire being. They think and feel differently so that their whole contribution is different but in a way that is entirely complementary to the other and such that, in marriage, they become 'one flesh' or 'one whole person'. This is true, however, not only in marriage but also in society as a whole so that whether we are married or not we complement one another, we enrich and fulfil one another, we keep one another sane!

However, there can be no clear definition of the role of men and women in marriage or in society. Christian writers such as Emil Brunner have attempted it - but they have been attacked, this time I believe rightly, by the feminist movement. There is a proper freedom in which, for example, you can have househusbands as well as housewives. Yet at the same time, men and women will bring something different to the same task - which is why Paul Tournier used to argue that we need female politicians who function as women and do not get squeezed into a male model.

Our covenant relationship with God is not controlled by systematisation and laws. We are called in covenant into a relationship with the living God who continually calls, challenges, commands through his living Word and Spirit and through his own Person. Any regularity to which we are called in daily obedience is not due to an abstract order or system or law. It is due to God being faithful to himself in his holiness and love. We must reject, therefore, any and all attempts to systematise the sexual orders, or roles, in marriage and in society. We must simply affirm, in accord with Scripture, that men and women are different and have a different contribution to make and we affirm, in accord with Scripture, that we cannot define nor yet definitely describe this differentiation. For we would be claiming for ourselves a knowledge of the will of God for a particular man and woman which we do not and could not have. God does and will lead men and women to serve in marriage and in society, in wonderful and unforeseen ways right outwith the defined systems that we have attempted to create for them.

3   Homosexuality

Scripture expressly forbids homosexual relationships. They are contrary to the natural order created by God. They are contrary to the Biblical doctrine of man and woman. The God-created, God-given, sexual differences of men and women, as already stated, are complementary and vital for true human fellowship, wholeness and fulfilment in marriage as God intended. These differences cannot rightly be set aside as they are in homosexual relationships.

According to Scripture man and woman in marriage are called by God to give themselves totally to each other in love. It is impossible for a man to give himself in the totality of his being to another man and likewise for a woman to give herself in the totality of her being to an other woman. Yet some maintain that homosexuals can give themselves in 'loving relationships which are non-exploitative, non-manipulative, equal'. That, however, falls far short of the totality of physical-spiritual self-giving of the one to the other in love which God demands in a Christ-centred marriage.

Some Christian leaders advocate a more liberal attitude to sexual relationships and want the Church to affirm 'the Christian value of homosexual unions which are reliable, permanent, honest, and exclusive, that is, non-promiscuous'. This argument is based on 'love' - but the idea of love is taken out of the Bible and then attached to something else; it is detached from the Person and saving work of Christ. The New Testament never speaks of love apart from the loving self-giving of God in Jesus Christ. Love was actualised in the atoning sacrifice of Christ through which he lovingly restores men and women into union with himself, heals the broken relationships between men and women and their fellows and lovingly heals and restores the marriages of men and women to that status in grace which he purposed from the beginning.

The practice of labelling people homosexual or heterosexual is modern, unbiblical and confusing. The Bible condemns homosexual acts, not, as sometimes argued, from proof texts such as the so-called 'sin of Sodom', which was gang rape, but because homosexual practice is against nature (Romans 1:24-27).

We all require healing. Scripture does not define us according to our sexuality, but according to our nature as sinners for whom Christ died.

4   Feminism

There is a helpful and Christian feminism which rightly seeks the acknowledgment of women's contribution to Church and society and their equality with men in dignity and status. This is to be welcomed and encouraged. There is, however, an extreme, militant, form of feminism which does not recognise and affirm the complementary nature of men and women in their personhood and contribution. It is this form of feminism which is so detrimental.

In affirming with Scripture that God created us either male or female, we are affirming that there is no other creaturely being other than male or female. Man and woman cannot transcend their sexuality. They cannot be other than the man and woman that God created them to be. They are in the depths of their being different from each other although complementary for their own and each other's fulfilment. They must not therefore aspire beyond their own and opposite sex to a third and supposedly higher mode of being who is neither man nor woman.

Yet the temptation is present in some quarters to aspire to become a human being who is neither male nor female, except outwardly and externally as if his or her sexuality as male or female was only temporal and provisional. It is not true to say as one woman once said to the present writer that the only difference between men and women is that a woman bears children and a man does not, for their sexuality is only accidental and therefore external! This, in a spiritualised form, is a movement of escape from sexuality and escape from what is really human. It is an attempt to deny our God-given manhood and womanhood.

No doubt, there are understandable reasons, intellectual, economic, social and political, which motivate such a desire by some feminists. However, we must insist there is no such thing as a being, or person, who as it were, is neutral and not entirely either man or woman. This kind of view really denies that man and woman find their fulfilment in marriage only in and through each other and together become one whole person. It is destructive to the marriage relationship.

In Matt 22:30 Jesus says that in heaven, men and women will no longer marry, but be like angels. Here, however, Jesus is speaking about marriage not about sexuality. He does not say that there will be no men and women in heaven. Nowhere does the Bible say that. It says that in the beginning God created man, male and female, and God does not reject what he has created. He affirms it, redeems it and exalts it. There will be men and women on this earth and in heaven for all eternity.

DIVORCE AND REMARRIAGE

Marriage is one of God's greatest and most joyful gifts. It is therefore tragic for the couple and for their friends and well-wishers, when some years (or even months) later, the happiness is gone, love apparently vanished, and the marriage ends in divorce. On average, at least 40 per cent of marriages in the UK end in divorce - the highest figure for any European country - and this is parallelled in the USA.

It is God's will that marriage should be permanent, a lasting partnership for life (Gen 2:24, Mark 10:7-8). In their togetherness, two become one whole person, reflecting in their relationship with each other God's relationship with his people. In their togetherness they reflect the image of God. 'Therefore,' said Jesus, 'What God has joined together, man must not separate' (Mark 10:9).

But divorce happens, in this sinful world in which we all live. So - despite God's desire for the permanence of marriage, is divorce theologically acceptable? Should the Church re-marry those who are divorced? These are questions with which the churches still wrestle and give different answers. We need to look at various passages both in the Old and New Testaments in considering this problem.

The Old Testament View

A passage in the Old Testament sometimes quoted in an attempt to try to justify divorce is Deuteronomy 24:1-4. 'If a man marries a woman who becomes displeasing to him because he finds something indecent about her, and he writes her a certificate of divorce, gives it to her and sends her from his house, and if after she leaves his house she becomes the wife of another man, and her second husband dislikes her and writes her a certificate of divorce, gives it to her and sends her from his house, or if he dies, then her first husband who divorced her is not allowed to marry her again after she has been defiled. That would be detestable in the eyes of the Lord'. This passage became the subject of strong debate in Rabbinic circles and has been much debated in Gentile and Christian circles.

Ideally the Jew hated divorce. God had said, 'I hate divorce' (Mal 2:16). The Rabbis had some important sayings. 'Unchastity causes the glory of God to depart.' 'Every Jew must surrender his life rather than commit idolatry, murder or adultery.' 'The very altar sheds tears when a man divorces the wife of his youth.'

Deut 24:1-4 simply says that if a woman has been divorced from a first and then second husband, or that second husband dies, she may not return and be re-married to her first husband. So this passage does not specifically authorise divorce and neither does any other passage in the Old Testament. Nonetheless by implication divorce is not ruled out. It is presupposed and accepted.

What is meant by 'something indecent about her'? Some, like the school of Shammai, understood it as meaning unchastity and nothing more. Others like the school of Hillel took a more open, permissive, view. It was their opinion that a woman could be divorced for many and even quite frivolous reasons, such as serving up to her husband a badly cooked or over salted meal! Sinful human nature being what it is, the majority of men in Jesus' day (a woman in Judaic law could not divorce) seemed to favour the more liberal, permissive, approach of Hillel to divorce. As a result despite the high ideals of Jewish teaching about marriage, in Jesus' day as in our day, marriage and the home were in danger of collapse.

The New Testament View

Jesus in the Sermon on the Mount made clear how the Deuteronomic passage should be interpreted. Jesus said, 'It has been said, Anyone who divorces his wife must give her a certificate of divorce. But I tell you that anyone who divorces his wife, except for marital unfaithfulness, causes her to become an adulteress, and anyone who marries the divorced woman commits adultery' (Matt 5:31-32).

In Mark 10:1-12, we have another, fuller statement where Jesus clearly condemns divorce. The Pharisees asked, 'Is it lawful for a man to divorce his wife?' Jesus replied, 'It was because your hearts were hard that Moses wrote you this law. But at the beginning of creation God made them male and female. For this reason a man will leave his father and mother and be united to his wife, and the two will become one flesh. So they are no longer two, but one. Therefore what God has joined together, let man not separate.' From these passages we can say two things.

First, it is God's will that the marriage covenant should be permanent. The breakdown of marriage together with divorce have no part in God's plan for the world. Marriage break down and divorce are grievous to God. Jesus affirmed that marriage is a call from God to life-long, indissoluble partnership.

Second, because of sin and the inability of men and women to live perfect lives in this world, the Bible in its teaching accepts divorce in certain circumstances such as unchastity.

The Bible sets forth the claims of the Gospel. It declares its high ideals in regard to marriage and in regard to the whole area of Christian life and conduct on this earth. We are called to accept these ideals. We are continually challenged by them and called to endeavour by the grace of God to live up to them. Any falling short of these high ideals is sin and for that we need constantly to be cleansed, forgiven and renewed by His Holy Spirit. Try as we may, however, no one can live up perfectly to these high ideals. All of us constantly fall short. Furthermore in this sinful disordered world where nothing is perfect we are frequently faced with a conflict of duties and responsibilities. In these situations we need to seek to carry through those responsibilities which we feel to be the greater. We need to choose to do what we feel to be the lesser evil, accepting that for us it is practically right in the situation in which we find ourselves. Yet in so doing we need to ask for God's forgiveness in our falling short and for his renewal of us. We are men and women living in a sinful world, who are saved only by God's grace, not by our living righteous lives. We are men and women who are utterly dependent on God's grace and need constantly through prayer to receive his grace, his guidance and renewal.

Because of our inability always to maintain the sanctity and permanence of the marriage bond, the Bible in its teaching accepts divorce, when we are faced with an irretrievable breakdown in marriage. In these circumstances divorce may be the lesser evil. At times it may be desirable, even necessary, for a couple to divorce. This does not mean the hallowing of divorce. For even in these circumstances divorce together with all that has led to it is still wrong. It is wrong even although in these circumstances divorce may be the lesser evil. In divorce, however right and necessary, both parties need the cleansing and forgiveness of God.

A Biblical Understanding

While the New Testament affirms and yet goes beyond the teaching of the Old Testament, our understanding of the Old is very important if we would understand the teaching of the New Testament and its application for our day. Paul gathers up the teaching of the Old Testament when he says in 2 Cor 6:14-16, 'Do not be yoked together with unbelievers. For what do righteousness and wickedness have in common? Or what fellowship can light have with darkness? What harmony is there between Christ and Belial? What does a believer have in common with an unbeliever? What agreement is there between the temple of God and idols? For we are the temple of the living God. As God has said: I will live with them and walk among them, and I will be their God, and they will be my people'. A Christian is commanded to marry only a Christian. Only so can he or she be a 'temple of the living God'. Only so can the Lord dwell with them and within them by his Holy Spirit and they together live in him and serve him. In the marriage of two believers the Lord is the foundation and cementing bond of their union. As such it is called to be permanent.

Our relationship with our marriage partner is called to reflect God's relationship with us. God does not reject Israel because she is unfaithful. He does not divorce her. His fidelity in Christ is our security. It is the ground and guarantee of permanence for all creation. As God is unendingly and unconditionally forgiving and loving toward us despite all our unfaithfulness toward him so we are called to be unending and unconditional in our forgiveness and love one toward another and toward the partner in marriage who may have been unfaithful. It is on the basis of God's faithfulness and unending love to us as well as the act of creation whereby man and woman in marriage 'become one flesh', that marriage is a call to life-partnership.

In this the New Testament is even more explicit than the Old Testament. 'Anyone who divorces his wife, except for marital unfaithfulness, and marries another woman commits adultery' (Matt 19.9). He 'causes her to become an adulteress, and anyone who marries the divorced woman commits adultery' (Matt 5.32).

In regard to adultery, it is important to consider what Jesus says in Matthew 5:27,28. 'You have heard that it was said, Do not commit adultery. But I tell you that anyone who looks at a woman

lustfully has already committed adultery with her in his heart.'
Jesus is going beyond the outward act of adultery. He is saying that
we can also commit adultery when we cherish adulterous sin in
our minds and hearts. Then we are just as guilty even although we
do not actually commit the outward act. Jesus reveals the nature of
sin in a much more radical way than does the Old Testament. When
we apply Jesus interpretation of adultery to what he says about
marriage and divorce, then the sin of an unchaste heart and mind
can cause an irretrievable break-down in marriage and lead to
divorce, just as much as the outward act of adultery. The sins of
the heart and mind are the main cause of marriage break-down.
The New Testament in this goes beyond what the Old Testament
teaches. It affirms but makes explicit what is implicit in the Old
Testament.

In this light it is helpful to compare what Paul says in 1 Cor
7:12-13, with what the Old Testament says in Ezra 9 and 10 and
Neh 13:23f. and Mal 2:10f. Paul says that a Christian husband or
wife must not divorce their unbeliever partner if that partner is
willing to live with them, although he does say, 'But if the unbeliever
leaves, let him do so. A believing man or woman is not bound in
such circumstances'. Paul is here speaking about a man or woman
who has come to faith in Christ and been baptised after they have
married. This is a different situation from a believer deliberately
marrying an unbeliever which as we have already noted the New
Testament forbids.

If we ask why New Testament teaching goes beyond that of
the Old Testament we can only say that it is due to the Incarnation,
death and resurrection of Jesus Christ. God has come. He has
entered into this world in a new and fuller way in Jesus Christ and
made his will more fully known and in Christ he gives us power
more fully to obey him. At the same time the Church which was
the believing community within Israel from Abraham's day and
even in the Old Testament embraced Gentiles like Rahab of Jericho
and Ruth the Moabitess as well as Jews, has been launched into the
world and become quite clearly an international community. The
success and fruitfulness of the Church would inevitably produce a
situation where one partner in marriage would be converted to
Christ while the other remained in darkness. In this situation the
unbelieving partner if he or she chose to continue in the marriage
presented an evangelistic opportunity and the Lord would give the

believing partner the grace and power both to remain faithful to Christ and to witness to the unbelieving partner in order to seek to win him or her for the Lord. And as Paul says, the other 'is sanctified' by the believing partner (1 Cor 7:14).

Deciding to Divorce

When Paul says in 1 Cor 7:15, 'But if the unbeliever leaves, let him do so', Paul is speaking of the unbelieving partner who remains obdurate in sin and who wants nothing to do with the Gospel and therefore does not wish to continue in marriage with a believer. Such an unbeliever could become a hindrance to the believing partner and might tempt the believer to depart from the Lord. Paul's recommendation here seems to harmonise with the concerns expressed in the Old Testament about an unbelieving or pagan partner turning the believing partner away from the Lord (in Ezra and Nehemiah believers were actually commanded to divorce their pagan partners).

The decision to divorce whatever the reason must always be for the people concerned an agonising and sad one. For a Christian it should only be taken after much prayer, thought and counselling.

The Church and Pastoral Care for others

Pastors must be very sensitive, compassionate and understanding of other people's problems, particularly when they are caught up in marital problems and sexual sins. The Church must avoid being judgmental. As God freely forgives all our sins in Christ, so God forgives our marital failures and sexual sins, however grievous. As the Church seeks to represent Christ to the world, she must seek to show the understanding, the compassion, and the love of Christ when encountering and seeking to help people in marital failure and break-down.

In regard to sexual sins, the Church, in order to be true to the Gospel and in order truly to help those who have erred, must stress that such sins are a breach of the covenant. They affect in the deepest and most personal way a person's relationship with God. They mar the image of God, they attack and spoil our relationship with God in Christ. Therefore they must be faced, acknowledged and repented of. The Church must lovingly help a person to do this, if that person would enter fully into God's forgiveness and be restored to union with Christ.

The Reformers rightly noted that the Old Testament distinguishes between what is called in the King James Version 'sins of a high hand' and all other sins, and that the New Testament accepted this distinction (1 Cor 6:13-20). In the Old Testament liturgy special ordinances and sacrifices were prescribed for the expiation of all other sins, but not for sins 'with a high hand'. For such as idolatry, murder, adultery and homosexuality, no liturgical ordinances or expiatory offerings were prescribed. They were sins against the covenant, the penalty for which was death. In that event the guilty person could only cast himself on the mercy of God. That was what happened to king David when he committed adultery and, by the sword of Ammon, murder. He knew that in his case sacrifice was of no avail (Ps 51:16). Hence he flung himself entirely on the mercy of God in contrite recognition that his sin was essentially against God. And God forgave him as he forgives every sinner, no matter who they are, when they fling themselves in utter contrition on his mercy. In Christ God has made full provision for forgiveness for every kind of sin including those of a 'high hand'; guilt is dealt with through the atoning sacrifice of the incarnate Son of God which is offered once for all on the cross.

Remarriage?

What should the Church do when someone who has been divorced asks to be remarried in Church?

Many ministers feel troubled when they receive this request and have spoken of their concern wondering what it is right to do in the circumstances. One minister in conversation with me recently summed up his and their concern by saying that he always feels uncomfortable when asked to re-marry a divorced person and yet feels uncomfortable if he does not re-marry! I share his feelings. With over forty years in the parish ministry I have wrestled with the problem endeavouring as far as possible in each situation to discover with the people concerned and in the light of Scripture the mind of the Lord. I have each time found the issue challenging and often spiritually rewarding.

We cannot approach any pastoral situation in a legalistic way. Equally in a particular situation we cannot expect to have a proof text set of guide lines. Frequently there are none. Our endeavour must always be to try and understand the teaching of Scripture as a whole and let that be our light and guide. We must be continually guided by Scripture's teaching on grace and salvation and be dependent on the Holy Spirit to apply the Word of God in a particular situation. In the remaining part of this chapter I will simply share with the reader what I have learned and endeavoured to practise.

Jesus said, 'What God has joined together, let man not separate'. As a Christian Church we cannot rightly say these words at a marriage service and then allow man in the form of the State to put them apart! This though is what some Churches or Christians seem to accept. In so far as God and God alone can join a man and woman in marriage, God and God alone can put them apart. This fact must control our understanding and all that we seek to do in marrying and re-marrying persons who come to us for help. We must endeavour to help a person or persons who have been divorced through the State to understand this, and help them to come to God in prayer with the request that God will put them apart from their previous partner, that he will forgive and heal and enable them to start life again.

It is always helpful to try in a compassionate way to know whatever is relevant and possible of the parties seeking to marry or re-marry. Only so can we in a loving way help the couple concerned. Many from their previous marriage have been carrying past hurts, feelings of rejection and guilt for which they need God's cleansing and deliverance before they can attempt to go forward into a new marriage. Both ministers and friends need to exercise great sympathy and understanding and be able to feel for them in their previous pain and rejoice with them in their hopes for the future.

I have never agreed automatically to re-marry a divorced person or persons. I have wanted first to try and explore with them something of what God is presently seeking to say to them. I have pointed out that as a minister I can marry them in the eyes of the State but I cannot marry them in the eyes of God. That is something which only God can do. A Christian marriage is not simply a union between two people, a man and a woman. It is a union between three, between man, God and woman or woman, God and man. If they want God to marry them and presumably this is why they want a minister to marry them in Church, then they must be willing to allow God to do for them and with them what only God can do. For that they must be willing in prayer to commit themselves and all that concerns them to God.

I have said to them that as a person or persons who have been married before, only God can put them apart from their previous marriage partner. They need God to set them free from their past and make them inwardly free to marry again, so that there are no hindrances or obstacles for their new marriage, nothing from their past to mar their future happiness. This of course is true of all of us no matter who we are or what our previous state. For all of us have sinned and until we have been cleansed, forgiven and delivered by Christ we carry the burden of our own sinful past. Only God in Christ can and does set us inwardly free. Marriage affects and changes our entire being. We become what we were not before. We become a different person. Each partner in marriage is instrumental in changing the other. We cannot of ourselves therefore separate from our partner in marriage without losing part of ourselves. If we would seek divorce, then only God can put us apart. If we would re-marry we need God as it were actually to re-make us and set us inwardly free and free from our previous marriage partner so that we are free to re-marry. Even the party who has more obviously been 'sinned against' carries a responsibility for the previous marriage break-down.

Therefore each person before entering into a new marriage needs to pray and receive God's cleansing and forgiveness for anything and everything in the past which they regret and which is wrong in the eyes of God. Unless and until people have so prayed and received God's forgiveness and transforming grace they are not free to re-marry. God has not set them free. The failure of so many to do this and to commit their past to God and to receive his forgiveness and renewal is a prime reason why the majority of divorces occur among those who have remarried.

Preparation for Remarriage

I always ask a couple who have asked me to marry them, and where one or both have previously been divorced, to have a time alone with God in prayer. I ask them to do this as soon as convenient after leaving me. I ask them, if they have not already done so, to commit to God the whole of their past and to ask and receive God's forgiveness for all that needs to be forgiven and to set them free. I ask each of them to do this but equally I ask them to do this aloud when they are alone and together. I ask them to commit their lives to God and then having done that to commit their present love and one another to God in Christ. I tell them that only if they can assure me that they have done this will I marry (or re-marry) them. Here I simply accept their assurance about prayer, about their asking and receiving God's forgiveness and about their commitment to him, in something of the same way that as a minister I would receive and accept a person's confession of faith when they take their vows in being admitted to communicant membership. God alone knows where they stand before God and how sincere they are. It is not for me or any minister to judge them. I simply accept their word and confession. I also like to pray with them along these lines.

A few couples after reflection have told me that they were not prepared to go further. They were not now prepared to be married in Church and would instead go to the registrar to be married. The great majority however have gone forward along the lines suggested and have expressed appreciation for the help given.

From the time that I was first requested to marry a divorced person or persons until I actually agreed to marry them has generally been not less than three months.

I have never married a person who confessed to being the guilty party in the break-down of their previous marriage. To my knowledge, such a person has not approached me. If however a person was manifestly repentant before God I do not think my approach would be different from my approach toward any other divorced person. King David in the Old Testament was certainly guilty of adultery and murder. He repented and God forgave him and must we not acknowledge that God may do so here? Any other approach would surely be legalistic and contrary to God's grace.

In agreeing to marry them I remind the couple of those two verses from two different Psalms in the Bible which are frequently, and in my own denomination regularly, quoted in the marriage service. 'Unless the Lord builds the house, its builders labour in vain' (Ps 127:1). 'Our help is in the name of the Lord, the Maker of heaven and earth' (Psalm 124:8). These verses make clear that if a house or home would be built secure then it must be built by the Lord. Without the Lord and his building there is no security. This is one common reason why so many marriages do not succeed. If the couple want the Lord to be the Builder and Maker of their marriage and home, then they must in prayer commit or re-commit themselves and their love to the Lord, ask him to put his seal and blessing upon them and on their love and their coming marriage.

I always ask the couple to set aside time every day throughout the whole of the rest of their lives to pray to God, to read his Word and to endeavour to worship God as faithfully as they can together in Church and together seek to serve him so that they allow God to preside over their marriage. I point out to them that in the marriage service in the Church prior to their making their vows to God, we pray together. In that prayer we give thanks to God for his grace enabling us to draw near and share in all his love and salvation. We give thanks to God for them both and for their love to each other. Then in prayer we commit them both to the Lord. We commit to him their love for each other and ask that as they take their vows to God, God himself will join them together as man and wife in the Lord. In so far as this is what we do in Church, then if the couple have already prayed together in this way prior to their wedding they can enter more fully and meaningfully into the service when we pray this way in Church. We then affirm that God has so joined them and affirm the words of Jesus, 'What God has joined, let man not separate'.

From time to time I have had some quite touching letters of appreciation in the months or years that have followed. I have seen a couple who were living together, after one had earlier been divorced because of a previous partner's unfaithfulness, come to faith in Christ. More than one couple after re-marriage have become very active and committed within the life and work of the Church.

Stoking the Fire

1 How is God the third person in a marriage? That is, how has marriage been understood as 'involving a relationship with God within the sacred bond of the covenant'?

2 How, then, is adultery 'an attack on God and his relationship with us and our partner in marriage'?

3 How does the Lord preside over Christian marriage and assume the 'responsibility for deepening our love and building our marriage'?

4 What is wrong with trying to rigidly define the roles of men and women in a marriage?

5 What is the impossibility in homosexuality? How do those arguing in favour of homosexuality 'detach love from the Person and saving work of Christ?'

6 What are the Biblical grounds David Torrance gives for divorce? What warnings to this permission does he assert?

7 What preparation for remarriage does David Torrance require and how do you respond to it?

8 Ultimately, how does God's covenant with us in Christ provide the deepest foundation and pattern for marriage?

Ignition Points

In Jesus, God became a particular man, a representative man, a Jew, belonging to that particular and most representative of all people, Israel. By so doing he confirmed that 'salvation is of the Jews' and that we are for ever indebted to the Jewish People.

God is for ever over-ruling the wrath of humankind and making it testify to him and praise him, even as by grace he over-ruled the terrible sin of human beings seeking to get rid of God for ever and putting to death on the cross the Lord of Glory.

Likewise God is over-ruling the unbelief of his covenant people today, as through them he speaks to the nations and confronts them with the Living God.

The Jewish People today who do not believe in Jesus as Messiah still belong to the Covenant People of God. They continue to be God's servant whom God is using as he confronts the nations and through whom he is speaking.

Our great longing and constant prayer must be that Israel will come to faith in Jesus as their Messiah and be saved in Christ, for their own sake and for the abundant blessing and salvation of the world.

We are to preach the Gospel to the Jew first and then to the Gentile. That is to say, our prayer and concern for the salvation of the Jews must lie at the heart of all our world mission today.

The whole history of the Christian Church and the long and sad history of Christian anti-Semitism, up to and including the era of the Holocaust and beyond that to the present day, means that our approach to them must be one of deep and sincere repentance and humility. Pray for the Jews every day.

Chapter Seven

THE MISSION OF CHRISTIANS AND JEWS

David W. Torrance

As the Church is challenged to answer 'Who is the real Jesus?' it is essential that we recall that the Jesus of Scripture is a Jewish man, a man born and steeped in the traditions, the history and the Scriptures of God's beloved people. In this essay, David Torrance illuminates how we cannot 'hear clearly what God is saying in Christ' without understanding the place of the people of Israel. He examines the election of God's covenant people, their place in the plan of redemption and the attitudes to which the Church is now called. Throughout, David Torrance joyfully reminds us that 'the Christian gospel was born within Judaism'.

The Gospel is the good news of the person of Jesus Christ, together with his teaching and saving work in his life, death, resurrection and ascension. It is the good news of atonement for sin, reconciliation with God and entry into the glorious new life of the Kingdom of God, in Christ Jesus. Jesus Christ is the self-revelation of God in the person, teaching and work of Jesus of Nazareth, in love and saving power for salvation of all who believe.

The Mission of the Church

The Church is called by her preaching, teaching and life, to make Christ known to the peoples of the world, in his person, teaching and saving work. The Church is called by her spoken word and by her life, to share this good news for the saving of the world. The mission of the Church is always God's mission even when by grace it becomes our mission. Therefore the Church must always so yield herself to Christ, in thankfulness, love and self-surrender, that God is able to reveal himself in Christ for the salvation of the world.

At first, in the New Testament era, the Church was small, being only a handful of apostles and other believers, all Jewish. Very rapidly the Church grew as Gentiles were added to the number of Jewish believers, until Gentiles composed the majority in the Church - as they do today. In every generation, the Church is commissioned to preach the Gospel, to the Jew first and then to the Gentile, making disciples of all nations and baptising in the name of the Father and the Son and the Holy Spirit.

The Mission of Israel

This was prior to the mission of the Christian Church as we know it. God called Abraham and made a covenant with him and with his descendants, in order that in and through them he might make himself known in love and salvation to the whole world and through them work out his covenant with all creation. God did not call the people of Israel and make a covenant with them simply for Israel's sake. God loved Israel. He also loved the world. He made his covenant with Israel, making them for ever his own people, so that in and through his special covenant with them, he might work out his purpose of salvation for the world. For God loves each one. Israel, then, is God's instrument, his 'servant', as the prophet Isaiah affirms, through whom God works out his redemption of the world. 'Salvation is from the Jews' said Jesus in John 4:22, meaning that God's purpose of salvation for the world, gathered up and accomplished in Jesus Christ, is mediated to us through the Jews alone.

That 'salvation is of the Jews' was true of Israel in the Old and in the New Testament era and it is for ever true. God revealed himself to his covenant people, in a way in which he has not revealed himself to any other people. To them were given 'the very words of God' (Rom 3:2), that is, God's Word, God's message, God's Law. Within Israel God did many great and marvellous things, many miracles, so that his power and his glory were made plain to the other nations. Israel, by God's grace and by God's calling, was a light to the nations. She had no light in herself. In herself, as Moses reminded her, she was stubborn and stiff-necked, sinful like any other nation. The Lord himself is the Light of the world. His Word given to prophets and priests down the ages of Israel's history was the Light. it was that same Word which became flesh in Jesus Christ, who testified saying, 'I am the Light of the world. Whoever follows me will never walk in darkness, but will have the light of life' (John 8:12). Israel as the bearer of the Word of God entrusted to her, testifies to the Light which in due course shone forth in fullness in Jesus Christ. Israel as the instrument through which alone the one true Light of God, the Light of Christ, is made to shine forth on the world, is thus called to be the light of the nations.

Through Israel's unique witness to the Word of God, we are given the Scriptures, in the reading of which we today, through the agency of Israel, are able to encounter God. In the reading and hearing of Scripture the one true Light of God is made to shine within us for our cleansing from sin and for our salvation.

In the New Testament era we have that central and supreme event of God himself coming into the world and in Jesus becoming a man - and for ever a Jewish man - for us and for our salvation. It belongs to the purpose of God that Israel was selected and by grace became a representative people for all the peoples of the world, so that in them we see ourselves before God and in God's dealings with them we see God's dealings with us. Jesus was that complete and perfect Jew who more than any other and in a unique way, is our Representative. In him we see and are made to understand ourselves and in him we see and understand God. He is the one who represents us before God in all our weakness and sinfulness and represents God to us in all his holiness and judgment and mercy. For Jesus is at once God and man. He is the one in and through whom, we, and all people, are reconciled to God. In him alone is there salvation.

In Jesus, God became a particular man, a representative man, a Jew, belonging to that particular and most representative of all people, Israel. By so doing he confirmed that 'salvation is of the Jews' and that we are for ever indebted to the Jewish People as God's servant for the redemption of the world.

From within Israel, God created by grace a small group of people, disciples, who were able by God's Spirit to recognise Jesus, who he was, to understand why he came, the meaning of his death and resurrection, the nature of his atonement and the pouring out of his Spirit at Pentecost, and who could therefore launch the Gospel into all the world. Hence the whole world is for ever built on the foundation of the apostles and prophets, all of whom are Jews.

What of Israel in the Post-Christian era? What of Israel today?

Christ has come and finished his work of atonement; the Gospel of salvation has been launched into the world; we have the Christian Church as the Body of Christ on earth, so is there any need for Israel as the servant of God? Is there any further place for her in God's purpose for the world? The answer of the Bible is a clear and decisive 'yes'. Israel continues to be, by God's eternal covenant of grace with her, his special servant, called to bring the knowledge of God and his blessing to the world.

The covenant which God made with Israel, like the covenant he made with all mankind and all creation, is God's covenant. It is a covenant of grace and God never breaks covenant. His covenant is not dependent on Israel's obedience or disobedience, her faith or unbelief. It is dependent entirely on God, on his enduring love and faithfulness to his purpose of love and salvation for Israel and for the world. His covenant is unalterable.

Some very sincere people wish to argue that the covenant with Israel has been fulfilled in Christ, so therefore it has been transcended, it has become universal, so that there is no further need for the covenant with Israel. Such people seek to argue thus: 'Christ has come and gathered up and fulfilled all that has gone before, the Gospel has been launched into all the world and the Christian Church is present, so there is now no need for God's covenant with Israel, it has been replaced'. They argue, 'Why go back to something lesser when we have something greater in Christ?'

By way of answer we can say - *First,* God's covenant with all humankind and with creation was prior to God's covenant with Abraham and his descendants. It existed long before. The two covenants, the inner covenant with Israel and the outer covenant with all humankind and creation, existed side by side inter-related all through the Old Testament era as they did in the New Testament era and do today. It is therefore not true to suggest that God's covenant with all humankind and all creation followed on after the covenant with Israel and replaced it.

Second, to argue that because God's covenant with Israel has been fulfilled in Christ, it has therefore been replaced, is to regard God's witness through Israel as a preparation for Christ and nothing more. That is to say the Old Testament Scriptures have value only as a preparation for Christ, so that once we have the full revelation of God in Christ they can if necessary be set aside or discarded. This however is wrong! The Old Covenant and the Old Testament Scriptures are indeed a preparation for Christ, but they are more. God is present and active speaking to his people then and now, through them. In and through them we can encounter God today and without them we cannot understand Christ clearly, nor yet hear clearly what God is saying in Christ.

Third, those who argue that because the covenant with Israel has been fulfilled, it has therefore been superseded, are not arguing in a biblical way. Nowhere does Scripture say or imply that in Christ and in the giving of the New Covenant, the Old Covenant is set aside and of no further use in the economy of God. Rather in the giving of the new, the old, although fulfilled and transcended, is confirmed and established in a new way. God's covenant of grace with Israel is an everlasting covenant, such that Israel continues to be God's instrument in and through whom he confronts the nations for judgment and salvation. Israel continues, whether believing or not, to be God's chosen people and a means of blessing to the Gentiles. God is over-ruling the unbelief which exists among his covenant people today, as among other peoples. Through them he still speaks to the nations and confronts them with the Living God.

Again, some people seek to argue thus: 'The majority within Israel rejected Christ and even today, the great majority of Jews do not recognise Jesus as Messiah and the majority of Jews are probably agnostic. Therefore they do not, and cannot, witness to God and his salvation in Christ.' This again, however, is wrong! God is his own witness to himself. God in his sovereign grace and power, is not dependent on men and women, nor on human faith, for the outworking of his purposes of love and salvation for the world. God is for ever over-ruling the wrath of humankind and making it testify to him and praise him. He is for ever over-ruling the sin of nations for his own glory even as by grace he over-ruled the terrible sin of human beings seeking to get rid of God for ever and putting to death on the cross the Lord of Glory. God over-ruled that most sinful event of all and made it his saving act for the world! Not only so, he made it his saving act from all eternity! Likewise God is over-ruling the unbelief of his covenant people today, as through them he speaks to the nations and confronts them with the Living God.

It is now time to ask: 'Who is this covenant people', these descendants of Abraham, whom God has called to be his servant for the saving of the nations? How do we understand their election?

Quite clearly there is an election within the elect people of God. Many people fail to recognise this and as a result much confusion arises. This two-fold election runs right through Scripture and lies at the heart of Paul's argument in Romans 9 to 11.

Paul says in Romans 9:4-5, where he is thinking of all Israel (the majority of whom did not believe), 'Theirs is the adoption as sons; theirs the divine glory, the covenants, the receiving of the law, the temple worship and the promises. Theirs are the patriarchs, and from them is traced the human ancestry of Christ.' Paul affirms that all Israel is embraced within this covenant.

Equally there is within Israel an elect minority. Paul speaks of them in Romans 11. There is Elijah and the seven thousand who did not worship the false god Baal. There are the prophets and priests who remained true to the Living God and faithfully testified to him. They are the true Church in the Old Testament era and in the deepest sense the true people of the covenant, the real Israel of God, of whom mention is made in Hebrews 11. They through faith and the Spirit of God were, like Abraham, reckoned righteous through the righteousness of Christ and were by the Spirit united to Christ, although they never saw him in the flesh or during their earthly life. To that number were added the number of the apostles and the company of believers who were filled with the Holy Spirit at Pentecost, together with the great company who have believed in Christ and will believe, all down the ages, until the last day when Christ will come to this earth in glory and gather his people to himself. In Christ, the Gentile believers are added to the inner elect of Israel, the true people of the covenant. By grace, in Christ, they are brought in and made to belong to the commonwealth of Israel, in which there are no nationalistic barriers of Jew and Gentile, for all are one in Christ Jesus (which is Paul's argument in Eph 2).

In the wider election of the people of Israel, the majority in Old Testament times and ever since to the present day, did not and do not believe in the living and true God who revealed himself in Christ Jesus. They, the unbelieving majority, nonetheless remain the elect people, who have been called as God's instrument and servant to show forth his glory to the world. This is what Paul argues in Romans 9 and again in Romans 11. God has not rejected his unbelieving people whom he has chosen. He has not broken his covenant with them because of their unbelief. It is utterly impossible that he should. Despite all unbelief and rejection of God, God maintains his covenant with them and continues to work out his purposes through them, as he manifests his glory to the world.

In Romans 9, Paul likens unbelieving Israel to Pharaoh and the Egyptians - a comparison that must have troubled Paul's fellow Jews. Pharaoh and the Egyptians refused to obey God. God loved them. He was patient with them. He gave them, time and time again, opportunity to repent so that they might share in the salvation of God and be blessed. With the smallest hint of a change of heart on Pharaoh's part, he answered Moses' prayer and halted the plague that was destroying Egypt. It was by going on and on rebelling against God that Pharaoh finally destroyed himself and the Egyptians. God however over-ruled Pharaoh's persistent rebellion and sin and used his very sin to display his own power and glory both to Israel and to the other nations of the world. Likewise, said Paul, in Romans 9, God has continued to over-rule the sin and rebellion of his elect people in order to make clear to the world his power, his mercy, his forgiveness, his judgment and his glory.

In this context, we may note that a very large part of what is recorded in the Old Testament and which makes up the content of Scripture is due to Israel's unbelief and rebellion. Because Israel was sinful and rebellious, so we sinful men and women today can identify with them and hear what God is saying to us in our sinfulness! Furthermore, it was Israel's sin and the Gentiles' sin, as represented by Israel's rulers and by Pilate, which put Jesus to death. God over-ruled that sin and used it to atone for this world's sin and to effect our salvation, thereby making even mankind's wrath to praise him. God over-ruled the rebellion of Israel so that Israel's sin became by God's over-ruling grace, the means of our blessing and salvation. This is what Paul says (Rom 11:11), 'Because of their transgression, salvation has come to the Gentiles', and again (v.12), 'But if their transgression means riches for the world, and their loss means riches for the Gentiles, how much greater riches will their fullness bring?'

The Bible constantly holds two things together, namely, the action of man and the action of God. This runs right through the Scriptures of the Old and New Testaments. On the one hand, Abraham in his freedom knew the Lord and obeyed him and on the other hand, God made himself known to Abraham and spoke to Abraham as a man speaks to his friend. On the one hand, Israel in her freedom did not know the Lord and did not obey God, and on the other hand, God held them back from understanding.

As Moses says in Deut 29:3-4 (a passage from which Paul quotes), 'With your own eyes you saw those great trials, those miraculous signs and great wonders. But to this day the Lord has not given you a mind that understands or eyes that see or ears that hear'. Paul gathers up this two-fold thought (the action of man and the action of God) when he quotes from Isa 29:10, '...the Lord has brought over you a deep sleep', and in Rom 11:7-8 he says, 'What Israel sought so earnestly it did not obtain, but the elect did. The others were hardened... God gave them a spirit of stupor, eyes so that they could not see and ears so that they could not hear, to this very day'. Again, there is the illustration of Pharaoh, to which Paul refers in Rom 9:17. On the one hand Pharaoh hardened his heart against God and, on the other hand, God hardened Pharaoh's heart. Pharaoh was a free agent. God gave him his freedom to obey God to the salvation of himself and his people, and God gave him his freedom to disobey to his own and his people's hurt. God's gracious calling of Pharaoh to obey in order that he and his people might enjoy the blessing of God's salvation, aroused Pharaoh to use his freedom to disobey God to his own and his people's hurt. God's very loving presence and his call to obey hardened Pharaoh in his sin.

Logically, we cannot hold together these two things: that Pharaoh hardened his own heart and God hardened his heart. We cannot logically hold together the action of man and the action of God. We can only hold them together in faith. In faith and in the living encounter between God and man, both statements are true. They are true to experience and to faith.

Put this in another way. We can say with Scriptural warrant, as we have done earlier, that when Pharaoh sinned, God over-ruled his sin in order to display his own power and majesty and glory, to all the world. When God's people sinned down through the ages, and when they put to death the Lord of Glory, God over-ruled their sin, so that by God's grace, as Paul says in Romans 11:12, 'their transgression means riches for the world'. Their sin, by God's over-ruling grace, became the means of salvation for the world.

Romans then is a thoroughly Jewish book and Paul is a thorough Jew. In his argument throughout Romans and in chapter 9 to 11, Paul is gathering up and reflecting the thought of the Old Testament. He is not confused or muddled in his thinking, as some have wrongly suggested. He is thoroughly consistent with the rest of scripture in what he says.

What of Israel today? Even today, the Jewish People, as a people, do not believe in Jesus as their Messiah. Many, perhaps the majority, do not believe in God. Yet they are still the covenant people. By what happens to them, God seeks to demonstrate his majesty and glory to the nations. They remain the Servant people, through whom God confronts the nations of today with the Person of the Living God and the Lord of history. They remain the means whereby God seeks to address the peoples of the world, challenging them to seek the Living God and the salvation of Jesus Christ.

In what way does God confront the nations and peoples of the world today through the Jews?

1 Their remarkable preservation through history, scattered as they have been across the world and persecuted time and again in the most horrific ways, points to the miraculous hand of God who has set them apart for himself and promised, 'Only if these decrees vanish from my sight,' declares the Lord, 'will the descendants of Israel ever cease to be a nation before me' (Jer 31:36). Their preservation points to the hand of God.

2 The very presence of the Jewish people today recalls us to their origins - to the great things which God has said and done in Israel and which are witnessed to in the Old and New Testaments.

3 The continuing presence of the Jewish people today - particularly their presence back in the promised land - reminds us that we and the nations have to reckon with a living, personal God. He is a God who acts in space and time, a God of judgment as well as mercy.

4 Their presence in the promised land reminds us in this twentieth century that our destiny is not in our hands. The nations do not hold their destiny in their own hands. It is not in the hands of their governments. Our destiny is in the hand of God who personally intervenes in history challenging the nations to humble themselves and to obey him, even as he challenged Pharaoh of old.

5 The modern history of Israel reminds us that God is over-ruling the continued sin of this world, as he fulfils his purposes of love and redemption. All history is leading up to the consummation of God's purpose for this world, when he himself will come in Christ and the nations must meet with him and render account to him.

Israel's return to the land of promise, following as it does an attempt under Hitler to obliterate everything Jewish, reminds us not only that God is the Lord of history but also that events seem to be moving on fairly fast toward the ultimate goal of history.

Israel continues to be God's covenant people and God continues to speak through the Jewish people and through them to show his glory to the nations and to all who have eyes to see.

What then should be the Church's attitude, today, to the Jewish people, that is, to the wider elect, who do not believe in Jesus as Messiah?

Gentile believers have been grafted in to the number of the inner elect of God's people. Together with Jewish believers they are the Church. The Church is comprised of all who believe. The Church reaches from Abraham to Christ and from Christ to our day and will continue until the day of Christ's return. The community of Jews and Gentiles who believe are above all God's servant called to make Christ known for the salvation of the world. What should be their attitude, our attitude, to the wider elect of God's people?

1 We must acknowledge that there has always been an election within the elect people of Israel. There has always been an inner and an outer elect among God's people, comprising those who believe and those who do not. Both groups of people are elect and have always been so. Therefore, the Jewish people today who do not believe in Jesus as Messiah still belong to the covenant people of God. They continue to be God's servant whom God is using as he confronts the nations and through whom he is speaking.

2 With Paul we must ever acknowledge our immense debt to the Jewish people. They have given us all our knowledge of God and of Jesus Christ. They have given to us that unique witness to him that is the Scriptures of the Old and New Testaments. We must acknowledge humbly and thankfully our continuing debt to the Jewish people today.

3 In praying for the Jewish people, we must pray that the veil be lifted from us and from all Christians so that we may acknowledge and love the Jews as God's uniquely chosen people, and that we cease to shame and dishonour the name of Jesus by our lovelessness to his own people, thereby making it all the harder for them to see Jesus as their Messiah.

4 We must pray with Paul earnestly and faithfully that the veil of misunderstanding will be lifted from the Jewish people so that they will welcome Jesus as their Messiah. and all Israel will be saved.

5 We must pray that God through his Holy Spirit will break down the barriers which separate the Church and the Jewish people (and which almost two thousand years of Christian persecution has done so much to perpetrate) and enable both to see Jesus as he is and hear his authentic voice and that both may recognise their need the one for the other in the fulfilment of God's mission to the world.

6 We must pray knowing with certainty that just as the sin of Israel was over-ruled and made a blessing to the world, so Israel's acceptance of Christ and their salvation will be for the world none other than 'life from the dead'.

7 We must with Paul anticipate the day when 'all Israel will be saved'.

What of our Christian witness to Israel?

We must share with Paul his deep longing for Israel to come to faith in Christ and pray earnestly that they might be saved. This needs to be emphasised today. This is important because many Christians, both evangelicals and liberals, persuaded that Israel continues to be the covenant people of God and is being used by God in his purposes of salvation, have come to the conclusion that Church and Israel must as it were go on in parallel in history, acknowledging one another, acknowledging that both are being used in the purposes of God but not seeking to influence one another for or against Christ: not until such a time that God on his own initiative reveals himself to the Jews as the Messiah (as he did to Paul on the Damascus road) and all Israel will be saved. This however is contrary to the whole spirit and teaching of the New Testament. The Christian Gospel was born within Judaism. Think of Paul's letter to the Galatians, where he deplores any attempt to detract from Christ and from salvation in Christ alone. He says to the mainly Jewish Church in Galatia, 'I placard Christ', and 'Let anyone who proclaims another Gospel be anathema'. Even in the context of Judaism, he insists that there must be no lessening of emphasis on Christ Jesus in whom alone is there salvation.

Again, think of what Paul says in Romans 10:1, 'Brothers, my heart's desire and prayer to God for the Israelites is that they may be saved.'

Our great longing and constant prayer must be that Israel will come to faith in Jesus as their Messiah and be saved in Christ, for their own sake and for the abundant blessing and salvation of the world.

Furthermore, we must learn the urgency of taking the Gospel to the Jew first and then to the Gentile. Take Paul's great concern for the salvation of the Jews and all that he says about the Jews, both in their sin and more so in their salvation being a source of blessing to the Gentile world; couple this with our Lord's command to go into all the world and preach the Gospel, first in Jerusalem, then in Judaea, and Samaria, and to the ends of the earth (Acts 1:8); or, link Paul's concern in Romans 9 to 11, with what Paul says in Rom 1:16, the Gospel 'is the power of God for the salvation of everyone who believes: first for the Jew, then for the Gentile'. Here we have the order for world mission, that is given to the Church for every generation. We are to preach the Gospel to the Jew first and then to the Gentile. That is to say, our prayer and concern for the salvation of the Jews must lie at the heart of all our world mission today. It must both theologically and practically influence and give direction to all our efforts to evangelise the world. We must seek to evangelise the world, in the faith and with the assurance that when the Jews come to faith in Jesus Christ then the full and abundant blessings for which we long and strive, will flow over in abundance to the rest of the Gentile world - and indeed, to the whole of creation.

Along with our responsibility to witness to the Jews, however, there is need for caution. Perhaps we should say that there is great need for Christian wisdom and love.

1 It is important to recognise that Israel continues to be the covenant people of God. They are therefore different from all the other nations and peoples of the world. We cannot possibly seek to evangelise the Jewish people as we seek to evangelise the other

pagan peoples of this world. The believing Jew believes in the same God as we do. The Gospel was born out of Judaism. Paul says (Rom 10:2), 'For I can testify about them that they are zealous for God, but their zeal is not based on knowledge'. Our approach to them must recognise this and be different from our approach to others. We must approach them as elder brothers who belong to the same family as ourselves, they by birth and we by adoption. Necessarily, we speak differently to a brother than to a stranger. The Jews are our brothers in spiritual things.

2 The whole history of the Christian Church and the long and sad history of Christian anti-semitism, up to and including the era of the Holocaust and beyond that to the present day, means that our approach to them must be one of deep and sincere repentance and humility. As Christians we have deeply hurt the Jews and in the past made it infinitely more difficult for them to understand Christ or want to come to Christ. Far too often, in history, the symbol of the cross has been for them the symbol of bitter hatred toward them and persecution. We need genuinely to ask for their forgiveness and seek reconciliation.

3 In our approach to them in Christ, we need to recognise more than we have ever done before, the terrible significance and hurt of the Holocaust. The Holocaust is now regarded as the third most significant event in the Jewish calendar. The other two events are the 'Exodus from Egypt' under Moses and the 'Fall of Jerusalem and subsequent Dispersion'. The Holocaust is regarded as the third most important event in the Jewish calendar, not simply because six million Jews (one third of their entire number) perished violently, but because it was an attempt to obliterate everything Jewish, once for all. Can we who are Gentiles ever begin to understand what that means for Jews today or what a deep impact it has had on both their thinking and their being? We cannot turn the clock of history back. We must not, we dare not, go back to the attitude which the Church had to the Jewish people before the Holocaust. In our approach to them in our concern that they should come to faith in Jesus as their Messiah, we must be aware of the reality of the Holocaust and the impact that it has had on our Jewish brothers and sisters, and should have on our conscience.

4 In our approach we need to go as those who have very much to learn from them; as those who are open and are ready to be taught and to change in our understanding and way of life. As Gentiles Christians, we need the Jews and we need believing Jews, in order that along with them we may grow up into the fullness of Christ.

How then should we approach them in Christ? Clearly, we need to witness to them of the things of Christ, not simply in words and perhaps not primarily in words, but in life, by our understanding of them, by our love, our repentance, our seeking of their forgiveness and our compassion. The Jews long to be loved. We all do. Yet with all their long painful history of being hated and persecuted, the Jews have very understandably a special longing to be accepted and loved. We are commanded in Christ's name to love them - to love them for their own sake in Christ and to love them for the sake of him our Saviour who became, and for ever is, a Jew.

In conclusion

Pray for the Jews every day. Pray that Jesus may make himself known to his own beloved people, and that they may know him and welcome him as their Messiah and be saved. Pray that the Church and the Jewish people be reconciled, for the fulfilment of God's mission to the world. Keep before you that great vision, which Paul has given us, of all Israel being saved and being an abundant blessing to the whole world. Think of all that this world owes to the Jews spiritually and physically. Think of their immense vitality and energy and brilliance, and their outstanding contribution to modern science and medicine (in which fields they lead the world) and think of all that energy and vitality being harnessed for the furtherance of the Gospel! Pray with that vision before you.

Stoking the Fire

1 What does the coming of Jesus mean for the debt the Church owes to the Jews?

2 What does Torrance mean by 'an election within the elect'? How does that apply to the way we think of Israel today?

3 What is the import of God's continual 'overruling' of human sin and wrath in the accomplishment of his purposes? What is the implication for Israel?

4 In what ways does God continue to use his chosen people Israel today?

5 How has the church historically blocked the Jews from seeing who Jesus is and from hearing the gospel?

6 What should be the attitude of the Church today towards the Jews?

Postscript by Jock Stein
THE LEGACY OF THE GOSPEL

The purpose of this chapter is to tell at least part of the story of the Torrance family, in order that readers may know a little of the people behind the writing, with particular reference to the impact and influence that the Gospel had on them, and through them on others. It is more an appreciation than a biography - for example, there is no discussion of the distinct and perhaps unexpected divergence of their political views.

I am grateful to the Revd Robert B.W. Walker, who came to know the family seventy years ago and subsequently married Grace, sister to the three Torrance brothers, for much of this account, and to his son Robert T. Walker for helpful comments.

Karl Barth comments in Church Dogmatics that the Biblical idea of the family is not father, mother, son, daughter but man and wife passing on the tradition of the faith to their children, who in turn pass it on to theirs. In the Torrances we have a remarkable instance of how the faith of one particular couple was passed on to their children by prayer and Christian upbringing.

The father, Thomas Torrance was born in 1871 in Shotts, Lanarkshire, Scotland and the mother, Annie Elizabeth Sharpe in 1883 in Richmond, Surrey, England. When presented with the Gospel, each embraced it joyfully, receiving and acknowledging Christ as Lord over the whole of life and saw themselves as inheritors of a sacred legacy to pass on to others. Annie Sharpe, an Anglican, began at once, and continued to the end of her long life at the age of 96, to tell others of God's love, and Thomas Torrance too, right up to his final brief illness at 88, did not cease to do the same - either in preaching which he loved doing, or in writing, or in talking to individuals whom he met, frequently leaving them with a Gospel tract.

In time, following the call which each felt from God to serve him as a missionary to China both underwent a course of training - the one as a minister and the other as a lay worker in the service of the Gospel. They both went out to China, under the China Inland Mission (CIM), as it was then - Thomas Torrance in 1896 and Annie Sharpe in 1907 - each doing wholeheartedly whatever work was assigned to them. After a while, Thomas Torrance was able also to give assistance in the work of the American Bible Society (ABS) to which he became more and more attached. Then, when back in Scotland and attending the renowned 1910 Edinburgh Missionary Conference, he was formally asked to take over the agency of the ABS for the large western province of Sichuan. This presented an enormous scope and challenge to his boundless energies and organisational ability and gave him a freedom not possible, under the circumstances, in the CIM. By now he had acquired a unique expertise in the language (Mandarin, spoken throughout the greater part of China), and was becoming increasingly recognised for his wide knowledge of Chinese history and literature, and as an authority on Chinese porcelain. He helped to establish the Museum of West China in Chengdu. Several of his collected items of porcelain and art were lodged in the British Museum and in the Royal Scottish Museum. His marriage to Annie Sharpe (or Betty as he called her) in 1911 gave him a greatly strengthened ministry, for she was completely at one with him in the work of the Gospel, offering constant support and encouragement, and adding her practical wisdom and other remarkable gifts to a union that, in daily devotion together and by the grace of God, brought faith in Christ to thousands of Chinese. A book by Annie Torrance, *How Shall We Train The Child?*, remarkable for its insight into how parents should bring up children in the faith, and written many years ago, has recently been published in the U.S.A., and is presently being serialised by Rutherford House in Edinburgh. One of Thomas Torrance's books is *China's First Missionaries*, in which he argues that the beliefs and customs he discovered of the Xiang tribes, in the remote Western mountains of the province of Sichuan, actually point to the tribes being of Semitic origin.

The work of the ABS under Thomas Torrance expanded rapidly and widely throughout Sichuan, involving many colporteurs and the training of converts to pass on the legacy of the Gospel to their own people. There is so much more one could say, but it would be outwith the main scope of this account. Suffice to say that in the last year alone of Thomas Torrance's almost 40 years in China the team he had trained had distributed over a million items - of Bibles, or parts of the Bible, or his own composed tracts and leaflets!

Thomas and Annie Torrance were blessed with six children, all born in China. Long before being born they were each solemnly committed to God for his service, with the prayer request that each would be actively involved in the ministry of the Gospel. The three girls, Mary, Grace and Margaret married ministers, and the three boys, Tom, James and David became ministers - all six in the Church of Scotland. Two of the girls served as missionaries with their husbands in Central Africa, and the third had a short spell with her husband in the Lebanon. There was a very special word in Deuteronomy which they sought to follow as parents: 'You shall repeat [these commandments] to your children, and speak of them both indoors and out of doors, when you lie down and when you get up.' Family worship was held daily, with a reading of the Bible and prayer. The children were encouraged to read through the Bible regularly for themselves, and to pray before and during their reading. A scheme from their parents - three chapters a day and five on Sundays - meant reading through the whole Bible once a year, and now in retirement one at least does so twice a year. When her eyesight was beginning to dim in the closing year or two Annie Torrance, anxious lest too much reading might hasten the process, confined her reading almost exclusively to the Bible, which over the years she must have read fifty or sixty times.

The oldest son was Tom, born in 1913. His early schooling was at Chengdu. Now his mother as well as his father was gifted academically: she taught Bible and English Literature at West China University. However she put no pressure on the children, and gave them no help with their homework, desiring them simply to grow up godly, with Christian values. One day Tom, age 9, skipped school. The head teacher came to the house afterwards and interviewed his mother; he said that Tom was stupid, and still didn't know his two times table. His mother accepted this - to such an extent that even when Tom was doing brilliantly at Bellshill Academy in Lanarkshire, she commented that she could not understand why teachers could give prizes to her son when he was stupid!

Tom continued with an ordinary MA degree, choosing not to take Honours so as to conserve limited family resources for the University education of younger members of the family. In any case he was anxious to press on to his Divinity studies, in which he graduated B.D. in Theology with distinction.

Tom went on to study and do a D.Theol. in Basel with Karl Barth, but had only been there a year when Prof. John Baillie was asked to recommend a Scot for a professorship in Auburn Theological Seminary (USA) for a year to 'pull them out of the doldrums'. So it was with some trepidation that Tom faced his first class of students, some of them much older than himself, and wondering what the youth from Scotland could teach them, but they soon learned to respect and appreciate him. On one occasion there was an interjection during one of his lectures. A student could not accept what Tom was teaching about the deity of Christ. When he received the typically direct and unexpected response that he did not believe 'because you do not want to believe' he was stunned into silence. For three days he fought with the issue, hardly able to eat or sleep, and then the light broke, as he accepted the diagnosis and became a firm believer. Needless to say, Tom's direct approach did not work with all students.

At the end of his time at Auburn other opportunities in the States presented themselves but Scotland beckoned, especially as he wanted to be back when the country was at war and after a session at Oriel College, Oxford, Tom was ordained, serving as a parish minister first in the Barony, Alyth and later in Beechgrove, Aberdeen. One of the elders in Alyth, previously accustomed to a nap during the sermon complained that under the new minister this was impossible! Between these two charges he served with the British Army in the Middle East and Italy during the war, as a Chaplain, and after demob had another semester in Basel after which he moved to Aberdeen, to his second charge. His ministries at the Barony and Beechgrove were both strengthening and fruitful, with a few from these congregations becoming ministers or missionaries. From Aberdeen he was appointed first to the Chair of Church History in New College, in the University of Edinburgh and then after two years moved across to the Chair of Christian Dogmatics - occupying the latter post for twenty seven years.

It is quite outside the scope of this account to list all the achievements over his long and still active life, or all those of his brothers, James and David, in their different paths. For example, Tom founded the Scottish Journal of Theology and presided over many academic Societies. He wrote many books, including *Theological Science* for which he was awarded the Templeton Prize for Religion. He spent one year as Moderator of the General Assembly of the Church of Scotland, he was awarded the MBE for war-time service, became a Fellow of the British Academy, and of the Royal Society of Edinburgh, and a Member of the Académie Internationale des Sciences Religieuses and its President for nine years, and the Académie Internationale de Philosophie des Sciences. Tom has travelled extensively throughout many parts of the world to preach, to give lectures, to attend conferences, to help initiate and formulate plans for new work. Yet when he came out of the army he told his mother, 'I'm not cut out to be an academic'!

James, born in 1923, and David in 1924, had all their schooling in Scotland, first in Bellshill and then at James Gillespie's School and the Royal High School in Edinburgh. When war broke out, James had his last spell at school in Maybole in Ayrshire, while David went first to Maybole, then to Blairgowrie in Perthshire, and finally back to the Royal High.

James' call up to the Armed forces, in the Royal Air Force, came when he was 20, his service throughout the rest of the war being in the South of England. It was then back to Edinburgh University to complete his MA studies where he became Senior Medallist in both Logic and Metaphysics and also Moral Philosophy, gaining a First Class Honours Degree in Philosophy. The Professor of Moral Philosophy, Prof. John Macmurray, at the end of his academic teaching life, once said of him to another professor that of all his students James had been the most brilliant. Following philosophy, in the Arts faculty, came his studies in New College, in the University's faculty of Divinity where he obtained an Honours BD degree with distinction in Theology. From there he went to Marburg in West Germany to learn German and then to Basel in Switzerland to study under Karl Barth, Oscar Cullmann, Karl Ludwig Schmidt and Walther Eichrodt. Thereafter it was to

Mansfield College, Oxford, primarily to study the works of John Calvin. Just before he left, his fellow post-graduates marched round the College grounds in procession, carrying tomes of Calvin rifled from James' room and singing with gusto, 'Calvin is my darling, my darling, my darling, Calvin is my darling, my darling O!' Finally, on returning to Scotland, he was ordained, entering into the parish ministry in Invergowrie, Perthshire, where he built up a large and flourishing youth work, with a most responsive congregation and where many were brought to faith in Christ. The Bible Class for example grew from under ten to over 75.

Yet he kept the common touch. Once, neighbouring clergy were invited to a church gathering in Invergowrie. One referred publicly to James' outstanding academic record. A woman member was present and heard this. 'I never knew our minister was such a clever man', she responded, 'When you talk to him, you wouldn't think he had a brain in his head!'

After a few years it was perhaps not surprising that, with his academic attainments, his obvious teaching abilities and strong Christian grounding and vision, all equipping him for the education of intending ministers of Word and Sacrament, he was appointed first of all to a Lectureship in the History of Christian Thought and then as Senior Lecturer in Christian Dogmatics, both in his old Alma Mater in the Faculty of Divinity in Edinburgh. After sixteen fruitful years there came his own Chair of Systematic Theology in King's College, in the University of Aberdeen for thirteen years - with a period as Dean - until his retirement in 1989. During this period, his son Alan was appointed to a teaching post in the same department - only because James' colleagues arranged the interviews behind his back, as he would of course never have allowed it.

For some years he was Convener of the Church of Scotland's Panel on Doctrine; Joint Chairman of the British Council of Churches' Commission on the Doctrine of the Trinity; Joint Chairman of the Conversations between World Alliance of Reformed Churches (to which he was a Theological Consultant) and the Lutheran World Federation; and also for many years Joint Chairman of the Joint Commission on Doctrine, of the Church of Scotland and Roman Catholic Church in Scotland. His publications include many articles on the Doctrine of the Trinity, on the

Theology of Worship, on John Duns Scotus, Calvin, Scottish Theology, Puritanism, Schleiermacher, Karl Barth, and in Dictionaries of Theology; and his book *Worship, Community and the Triune God of Grace*. Since retirement he has been involved to a great extent in many lecturing and preaching tours abroad and intends now to devote his time to further writing on such subjects as worship, prayer and the Trinity, and to prepare to give the Warfield lectures in Princeton.

David, in his University career, gained an Honours MA degree in Philosophy (being awarded the senior medal and prize in Logic and Metaphysics) and an Honours BD degree in Theology with distinction, both in Edinburgh, the latter in New College. The former studies were interrupted by World War II, for he joined the Army and spent his whole period of war service of nearly four years with an Indian Division, in India. Here he experienced some difficult times, but kept his sense of humour, being greatly amused on occasion with the methods adopted and the terminology of commands, instructions and explanations used by some, senior in rank, as they tried to instil army knowledge into assumed ignorant 'juniors', some of whom were far more intelligent and of higher educational attainment than they. It was a time though for which he came to be deeply grateful, a period when he had ample opportunity to meditate on the deep things of God, on what he had learned at home and come to love of the Bible, on the real issues of life and on what God wanted him to do with his life. It was a time of increasing maturity - a time that helped him over his natural shyness - critical, formative days.

Following his return to Scotland and before he started his main work in the full time Parish Ministry there were very many occasions both before, during and after his University days when David was engaged in Missions - with the University Christian Union, with New College, with D.P.Thomson and 'Tell Scotland', with Billy Graham, counselling and training counsellors. There were also the many years when, during his Parish Ministry, he led Church of Scotland Seaside Mission teams in different resorts - sometimes large teams up to sixty members and even, on one occasion of a hundred including part-timers. Many came from each of his own parish charges. There were many who found strengthening in their Christian life and witness through these missions, or came to believe and rejoice in the love of Christ, and several are now in the full time ministry of the Church. When offered a teaching post in Scotland he declined, not feeling a call to this work. Later when invited to teach theology on three different occasions in Africa he accepted the invitation, but unexpectedly the door closed.

It is interesting that each of the three brothers effectively became 'dux' of New College, being awarded the Senior Cunningham Fellowship, as assessed over the whole three year period of their Divinity course. Yet all three had the experience of being thought unintelligent - Tom by his headmaster in China, James by a parish member, and David by his session clerk: after a whole year in his first parish, his local school headmaster came up to him and asked, 'Have you ever been to university?'

There are other interesting similarities. All three have been beekeepers and skiers, all were in the parish ministry of the Church of Scotland, all are both evangelists and theologians, and each has had to a greater or lesser extent a ministry overseas. Each has married into the medical profession - Tom to a nurse, Margaret Spear; James to a doctor, Mary Aitken; David to a doctor, Elizabeth Barton. Each has been blessed with a wonderfully supportive, gifted wife, and husband and wife have been very much at one with each other in life and work, a harmony in marriage which is a telling example and witness. Each has a family of three, all committed Christians, and with one from each family in the full-time ministry of the Church. To each the present writer owes more than he can say. Tom and James have a further similarity in that each has had a Festschrift published in his honour.

It is not within my remit to present any detailed theological assessment, even were I able, but to say something about them as people and to assess briefly their contribution in the work of passing on the legacy of the Gospel, both to their children and friends and to all who have heard them or read their works. Though indeed gripped by the Gospel, they have never been exclusively bound up with purely theological matters and out of touch with the real world. This has enabled them to see some of the implications of the Gospel and on occasion to have an impact on social and political issues, on matters of justice and compassion. I hope to give a few practical examples of their actual life, upbringing and character.

Each would acknowledge the great sense of debt they owe to their parents who from their earliest days, and even before birth, prayed for them as already mentioned, and prayed with them in daily family devotions and taught them to love the Bible and to read it daily for themselves. They came to believe strongly from their parents that God really did speak to them through its pages, as they laid themselves open to listen to him, to hear who he was, what he had done in Jesus for the world , how they should live and work for him under his leading. God for them really was present and they were secure in his love. It was in such an atmosphere they received the legacy of the Word, and appropriated it with a happiness that has never left them. Early they were encouraged to read books, and such as Robert Bruce on The Sacraments, Luther's Commentary on Galatians and many of the great missionary classics, were read while still at school. These were enjoyed and made a great impression. There was never at any time academic pressure to do well at school, and they grew up as a happy united family.

Tom had the privilege as a boy when still in China of accompanying his father on some of his itineraries, in the work of the American Bible Society, especially among the Xiang tribes in the high far Western mountains, selling or giving out Bibles or selected portions, preaching and conversing and seeing the joy of Xiang and Chinese coming to believe in Jesus. He saw too how often mere reading of the Bible, with no one to explain or interpret, brought new life in Christ. His boyhood ambition was to become like his father one day and tell others the same good news and we know that later he had an intention to return to China as a missionary. His love for them took him back there in his late 70's and even once when over 80. He paid three visits to the city of his youth, the city of Chengdu and also to the Xiang people, meeting some who remembered his father, with a gratitude and affection that had lingered for well over forty years! Part of his mission was to give support to the Church in Chengdu, as well as to encourage the Xiang people to rebuild their Church, (and not just Church buildings or Gospel houses) for in the great Communist thrust for power that swept initially through the province of Sichuan the Xiang Churches had been wantonly destroyed and their Pastors, with all their sons except one, ruthlessly slaughtered. On one of these visits he carried with him the title deeds of a Church that his father had brought to Edinburgh for safe keeping when the Communists began to threaten the area.

In his late teens, Tom engaged with a friend in a mission in South Queensferry in the open air under the shadow of the Forth railway bridge. Audiences were generally meagre, but they preached nonetheless, even when they could see no one listening. One of the results of the mission only came to light about forty year later, when an old lady in Aberdeen told David that she and her husband, both chemists, came to faith in Christ through that mission. Other formal missions took place both in and outwith University life. Some students in the course of their studies for the Ministry, had a conversion experience, sometimes through a lecture, sometimes through personal conversation with him. His influence on others ranges from the Art College student (now my wife) who went to New College after hearing Tom speak to her Christian Union, to the current Chaplain to the US Senate (where, incidentally, you can find Tom's portrait).

Tom is widely known for his forceful proclamation of the staggering fact of the incarnation of the eternal God, and for his stress on the entry of the eternal Son into the darkness and shame of our situation, into the very midst of our rebellion and alienation, and taking our place in order not only to bring forgiveness but also to renew and restore our humanity in his own perfect humanity. The three brothers in their different ways have stressed the need for the Church to hear anew of the uniqueness of Christ, his offering to the Father for us, through his whole life and death and on into resurrection, a perfect obedience in holiness and faithfulness. In his resurrection and ascension to the Father in our humanity he has raised our human nature to participate in the eternal communion he enjoys with the Father and the Spirit. He then sent his Spirit to lift us up to participate in his victory and resurrection, and in his own communion with the Father. The Spirit is given to lift us up to Christ, to share in him and to open us up to knowing him. The Spirit thus unites us to Christ and at the same time unites Christ to us, making us know his presence with us. Then as our Great High Priest ever interceding for us, Jesus enables us in the Spirit to participate in his ongoing intercession and mission to the world, assuring us of the final consummation of all things in him when he comes again in power and glory. In all these emphases the underlying conviction throughout has been, as with James and David also, the joyful certainty of God's self-revelation in Christ, without which we can only vainly speculate as to what God is like.

Alongside Tom's influence and attainments there is also a human touch and kindness that is ready to reach out to any who may need help. With his students there were occasions when Tom spent considerable time visiting them in hospital or patiently counselling them and answering their questions.

James too has made a very special contribution, from his own appropriation of the legacy of the Gospel, both in Scotland and in many parts of the world. In his earlier years, both as a student and post-graduate he was engaged in various missions and as IVF representative led a number of these in Scotland. Many of his students, in Edinburgh and in Aberdeen look back with gratitude for their days under his tutelage when what they learnt in their understanding of the Christian faith became the groundwork and vision of their whole future ministry. Almost universally their tribute to James would be of the extreme lucidity of his teaching and of how much easier it was, than with most other lecturers, to take away the gist of a lecture, and to retain salient points of thought.

Travel overseas as visiting Professor has been extensive and was undertaken frequently both when in New College and King's College, Aberdeen, but has continued even more widely since retirement. Visits to theological seminaries and colleges, congresses, conferences and numerous churches throughout many areas of the United States and Canada, New Zealand and Australia, as well as South Africa and Northern Ireland, sometimes for extended periods of two or three months, and even to Western Samoa, are so well received that he is repeatedly asked for a return visit. Many ministers have found their whole ministry transformed through new insights into the Gospel of unconditional grace and the continuing intercession of Christ, as expounded in his book, *Worship, Community and the Triune God of Grace*.

When the Gospel of Christ lays hold of a man or woman it gives a readiness to speak the truth and often an incisive insight into social or political circumstances. During the apartheid years when James was in South Africa during four extensive tours he frequently met staunch supporters of the apartheid system, ready passionately to defend their position, even Biblically. In any critique of the system James took a clear Christological line during the many lectures he gave, in different Universities, in Dutch Reformed Colleges, in an International Calvin Congress. He would say that to hold out Jesus Christ to the blacks and coloured was 'not only to hold out forgiveness and salvation, but to give them their humanity and dignity'. The Incarnation meant that Christ had 'assumed our humanity, be we black or white, male or female, sanctified it, offered it to the Father without spot or wrinkle to be given back to us', and that thus God commits us to seek justice and equal rights for all. Tom in his short visit to South Africa during his term as Moderator was equally forthright, as he met prominent ministers of the Dutch Reformed Church - who for the most part supported apartheid. He also met among others the Prime Minister, and spoke so straightly to him that he said no one had ever spoken to him like that before, meaning perhaps that no one had ventured to do so. For James there was only one way for South Africa, among many proffered solutions, to solve the extraordinarily difficult problem of apartheid and his was the way that was eventually taken. David, who has a wide knowledge of the Jewish/Arab divide, was once heartily scorned by an official of the Church for suggesting, years before the 1991 War to relieve Kuwait, that the immediate key then to events in the Middle East was Iraq. That insight appears even more valid today!

James, with Tom, has been instrumental in introducing many to John McLeod Campbell, and particularly to his recently reprinted classic, *The Nature of the Atonement*.

One of the great issues, he points out, of the book was the currently accepted teaching of limited atonement - one of the main issues that brought about Campbell's deposition from the ministry of the Church of Scotland in 1831, for his opposition to it. More than 160 years later James was prohibited by the interim moderator from occupying a pulpit overseas during a vacancy - much to the dismay of many in the congregation - because he too did not adhere to the doctrine, holding as vigorously that Christ died for all and not just for an elect few. An opportunity then arose for him to address a large packed audience from the congregation on the title of a paper given earlier to the Calvin Congress, *The Concept of Federal Theology - Was Calvin a Federal Theologian?* At this gathering he argued that John Calvin never taught a limited atonement and said that if a Church refused ordination to anyone not holding to this doctrine, then it would not have been willing to ordain Martin Luther, or John Calvin, or John Wesley!

James' emphasis on the continuing intercession of Christ came up unexpectedly one day when, as James was taking a dip on a Pacific beach, a gentleman came walking along, surprised at someone venturing into such cold water. They introduced themselves and it soon transpired that the gentleman was in a state of deep sorrow. His wife whom he loved dearly was dying of cancer. He was at that moment trying desperately to pray but was too distraught to know how to pray. His father had been a minister but he himself had drifted away from the Church. He used to pray but now found this impossible. James took him at once to Christ and certain passages of Scripture and said very simply that Christ was praying for him. He then prayed with him there on the beach. Would James, he asked, be willing to come and meet his wife and tell her the same thing that had so completely lifted his own spirit? He gladly did so, praying with them both. Some time later a letter came to say that the last remaining days together of the devoted couple had been wonderful ones in the sure knowledge of the abiding love of God.

Another theme upon which James has laid great emphasis is that of the Trinity, endeavouring to recall the Church back to its roots in this vital issue - a subject to which Tom himself has contributed so much in thought and in writing over the years, and with which David too is in full agreement. It is James who tells us that the renowned Bishop Lesslie Newbigin, on his return from many years in India, once said that the Church in the West had largely lost the great doctrine of the Trinity, and that there was a great need for the recovery of this, the Faith's ultimate foundation. As a result of the Commission, in which James was a co-Chairman, of the British Council of Churches on the Doctrine of the Trinity, representing all the major British Churches, three booklets were produced on *The Forgotten Trinity*. James has often written and lectured too on the issue of federal theology and its adverse influence on the thought and life of the Church. Other abiding emphases have been on the vicarious humanity of Christ, and particularly on the fact that God is a covenant-God, not a contract-God - a contract, in common parlance, being in his words, 'a legal relationship in which two people or two parties bind themselves together on mutual conditions to effect some future result', while 'theologically speaking, a covenant is a promise binding two people or two parties to love one another unconditionally'. It is possibly here in driving this point home so continually and lucidly that James has had his greatest influence.

While the ministry of Tom and James has been largely in the field of academic teaching and lecturing, that of David has been predominately in the pastoral ministry with great emphasis on the practical ongoing mission of the Church, both here in Scotland and overseas.

Mention was made earlier of formative days for David in the army. At the end of the war he was still in India, with troops in a jungle division. He would soon have to make up his mind about his future and now he had to face what he had for so long felt to be the call of God to enter the ministry. He tells us he resisted this call persistently and strenuously, so much so that he even hoped at one point that he would not return from the war for he knew that then God would place him in the ministry. He would do anything to serve God but this. In prayer he offered to God to return to India as a missionary doctor and help the poor. He did not particularly want to be a doctor but was more willing for this if only to escape from the increasingly pressing, even terrifying call to be a minister. Three long days of 'turmoil' followed when he felt 'torn apart' and then alone in his tent felt in a strange but powerful way that God was there with him, almost as if he could touch him, and still calling insistently. Still he resisted but then such an alarming word came to him, telling him that if he refused he 'would never again have peace or joy', that he was utterly shaken. Kneeling there on the bare earth in the tent he prayed, 'All right Lord, I will enter the ministry, but it is your look-out!' It was, he says, a disgruntled prayer but then 'a miracle happened'. He was immediately filled with 'incredible joy and peace' and that 'joy of being a minister of the Gospel has never left me'. He returned to Scotland not only reconciled to becoming a minister but looking forward to it.

In assistantships both in Broughton Place Church, Edinburgh and in St. Mary's, Haddington, he worked with young people, and from the congregations some entered the ministry and others into mission work overseas.

All three bothers could be very direct in sharing the Gospel. In a mission once in the North of Scotland a retired major general in the army, on agreeing that serious disobedience of orders would involve a court-martial, was told that through disobedience in not attending the worship of God he was 'guilty of an act of rebellion and would be summoned to a court-martial by none other than the King of Kings'! Some months later David received a lovely and gracious letter enclosing a generous donation to the work of mission. The officer had not forgotten the conversation!

Tom's memoirs of his visit to the Middle East in 1936 (after gaining the Stuart Blackie Travelling Fellowship in Greek, awarded to study Biblical languages and archaeology) or of experiences in Italy during World War II contain several hair-raising escapades. Were the daily prayers of his parents at home and other members of the family a factor in his coming home alive? A poisoned drink which he was fortunate to bring up, attacked a few times with a knife or other lethal weapon, a revolver thrust at him by an Arab accusing him of being a Jew, suddenly arrested in Iraq for 'spying' just after seeing bodies hanging up by their necks and then himself being sentenced to death, transported to Baghdad under police escort and finally deported to Syria - these are among some of the escapades.

The strangest of circumstances sometimes became the opportunity to plant the seed of the Word. By a stream one day up on the slopes of Mount Olympus and close by the Monastery, where he had had a quiet cell for the night, he was having his devotions. Along came an old monk hobbling with the aid of a walking stick. He inquired what Tom was reading and became deeply excited, hardly able to believe his eyes when he was shown a Greek New Testament. All they had apparently in the Monastery was a Lectionary. Although the monk protested at his kindness Tom gave him the Testament. The next day after climbing Mount Olympus alone he found the monk again, by the stream absorbed in his new treasure. He appeared 'completely transformed, for an inward light seemed to illumine his whole person and shine out of his eyes. That was the quickening and enlightening power of the Word of God of which I had known as a boy in China'. The experiences of that visit, over 60 years ago now, remained with him throughout his later service in the Gospel. When he left for Athens they exchanged walking sticks, Tom being given a walking stick of stout mountain ash, which he used later in his pastoral visitation.

In Italy during the war, against the advice and in spite of the anxiety expressed by the Officer in command, Tom insisted on being with the soldiers at the very front of the advancing action. He was with the Church of Scotland Huts and Canteens, stationed with the unit and with a vehicle fitted for the purpose. Once he crossed through no-man's land to obtain a suckling piglet to give some cheer to the 'boys' at Christmas, acutely aware on the way back that grave consequences could follow a squeal! He was frequently exposed with the forward troops, not only to their rough conditions but to the deep horrors and tragedies of battle, having men near him, and once on either side of him, blown to pieces and having to gather up what was possible for burial and conduct the funeral service at the spot. At times he had to attend to the wounded, or speak to dying men as guns on either side blazed away, and lead them to faith and peace in Christ, celebrating the sacrament of the Lord's Supper sometimes just where the men were in the open air. His soul revolted against the frightful slaughter all around, and his brother-in-law vividly remembers a letter received in Malawi at the time telling of the appalling carnage he was witnessing and how he might have been tempted to give up belief in a God of love but for the Cross of Christ that spoke louder than all the thundering guns of destruction. He found numerous opportunities to speak of the faith and often found that many, hitherto irreligious, were now, in face of the utter fragility of life and with peril so close at hand, open to the Gospel and ready to respond to the gracious word of the love of God. Tom came back deeply affected by the war, but with the incarnation and the theology of the Cross burned even more deeply into the centre of his thinking.

Fortunately David was not called to active warfare either in Europe or the Far East, though James saw something of the onslaughts and damage inflicted by the Luftwaffe in England. David was ordained as a minister of the Church of Scotland in 1955 and over a period of 36 years held three charges in all till his retirement in 1991 - Livingston in West Lothian, Summerhill in Aberdeen and Earlston in the Borders. There was an outstanding Biblical ministry in each of the parishes, where in each he was greatly loved, found many lives were changed and many deeply grateful for all he

meant and taught. As a friend and counsellor, and not just as a
father in the faith to many, he was sorely missed at each demission.

One day as David stood on the pavement outside the Church
Offices in Edinburgh he was suddenly arrested with the words,
'Are you a holy man?' Standing before him was an Indian.
Suppressing the temptation to laugh, for the face of his questioner
was so serious, he replied, 'Well, I try to be'. The Indian then told
his story. He had been brought up in India as a strict, practising
Hindu. He had come to Scotland to study engineering and while at
University had come to faith in Christ. At first and for some time
he was full of tremendous joy and recently all the joy had departed.
'What is wrong with me?', he asked. He was told only the Lord
knew. David however said he might make some suggestions. Might
it be lack of prayer, neglect of reading the Bible or of not continuing
in Christian fellowship.... or some other reason such as failure to
forgive someone who had wronged him? 'That's it! That's it!', he
broke in excitedly. On being asked what he meant he said that
someone had done something which hurt him and he could not
forgive that person. He was told that inability to forgive would
come as a barrier between him and God and would certainly take
away his previous joy in the Lord, that we can only receive God's
forgiveness if we are ready and prepared to forgive others what
they may have done.... that forgiving others is frequently not easy
and we need to ask God for the grace to forgive. Could he do that?
He agreed. So standing there on the pavement they prayed, asking
God to help him and give him the grace to forgive his friend. A few
days later a moving letter came to say that he had gone off, sought
out and forgiven his friend, and all the joy of the Lord had returned.

Further interests for David have been in the movement for
Renewal in the Church through the Holy Spirit, also in the ministry
of Healing and in God's purpose for the Jewish people. He believes
it is in God's strategy for world mission that we must seek with
Paul to take the Gospel 'to the Jew first', in the understanding that
the coming of the Jews to faith in Christ will result in a great forward
advance in world mission. He has served and still serves on a number
of Committees of the Church, and contributes to the activities of
Christian organisations, societies and conferences. A number of
his articles have appeared in print or been incorporated in the books
he has edited. A major work was the organisation and editing, along

with Tom, of the translation from the original Latin into English, of all Calvin's commentaries on the New Testament - twelve volumes in all. He has also contributed to and edited *God, Family and Sexuality* and similarly *The Witness of the Jews to God*. He is in constant touch with and involved in giving encouragement to 'Messianic Jews' - Jewish believers in Jesus as the Christ - who as he tells us now have many congregations, especially in Israel and in the United States. He wrote the booklet, *The Mission of Christians and Jews*, and co-authored with A.F. Lamont, *Anti-Semitism and Christian Responsibility*.

David has written of his special indebtedness to his mother, especially during the years between the ages of four and eleven when his father was on his own in China for his last term and the family were back in Scotland. Indeed all the children share this sense of enormous debt. Tom has said that she was *the* theologian of the family. Not only did they imbibe from her her love of the Bible but a great deal of her understanding of the message of the Word and its meaning for them and the world. She gave them a foundation in theology that became the grounding for their own and a love of the Gospel which became theirs to pass on. Their father too had a great influence both before and after this period, in part from his weekly letters to them from China. The whole thrust of his work told how he loved the Word but they knew this too through the way he spoke of it at home. At one time he knew by heart, both in English and Chinese, the whole of the Psalms and also much of the New Testament.

There is no doubt that each parent had a remarkable trust and understanding, and that together they provided a home and Christian upbringing which has made a deep and indelible impression on the whole family. If the Torrance brothers inherited a deep commitment they still had to make it their own, think it through in the context of their own century, and pass it on. Here Tom, in a sense, being ten years older, was the pioneer, equipping himself with a knowledge of the Fathers, the Reformation and of the history of Christian thought and relating the substance of the Christian faith, incarnation, atonement and resurrection, to movements in modern thought, particularly in science. Here he has indeed made a lasting contribution, pointing the scientist to the importance of theology, pointing the Church to the relevance of science. With his breadth of knowledge and incisive understanding he often went right to the heart of an issue as he saw it and made his own position plain. Like the horse in Job who could smell the heat of battle afar off Tom was usually first into the theological fray! He stated things exactly as he saw them and while not meaning to wound very often he did so by being so forthright. An attack on an argument could be taken personally when it was not intended to be. And yet behind all the intense energy of his thought there lay, as J.S. Stewart said, a childlike faith. Tom prayed his theology, and when he began each lecture at New College he always opened, as did James, in a short prayer, which was a beautiful summary of the whole lecture. Some of his finest writing is contained in his two little books of sermons where his theology is distilled into simple language. Tom's intellectual contribution has been massive, and his influence may well grow greater in time. Hitherto he has often been listened to more abroad than at home, but it is to be hoped that even when people are grappling with some of his more difficult concepts they will remember that they should not be divorced from prayer or from the heart.

If Tom has been pioneer, James has been the consolidator, in close agreement with Tom's theology but adding his own considerable insights and focussing particularly on what he has felt have been the most critical areas of the Churches' understanding, the need for a return to the unconditional nature of God's love, the role of the humanity of Jesus in our salvation, and the continuing priesthood and intercession of Christ. If Tom has written on the whole range of Christian doctrine, James has focussed in his teaching on the very heart of the faith for ministers and laymen. His whole approach has been eirenic, attempting to win people, conscious that controversy can alienate them, and that through patiently unfolding the unconditional nature of grace agreement can follow. James too is no stranger to controversy, and has been uncompromising when he has felt fundamental issues have been at stake. In his preaching, as in his dealings with people he has endeavoured to reflect the unconditional love of God. In that he has exercised a considerable influence, not only here in Scotland, but wherever he has lectured abroad. It is frustrating that he has not written more.

David, as a theologian in his own right, could easily have gone also into the academic world, but felt called to the pastoral ministry, giving particular emphasis to mission. While again sharing the same theology he has applied his knowledge of the Bible to the man or woman in the pew, to people in the ordinary tasks and situations of life, work, marriage, sickness, bereavement, and to the person outside the Church in parish visitation and mission in general. He too has been widely appreciated. There is a bulldog in his nature when it comes to standing for a truth or in contending for an issue in which he believes, and once he gets the bit between his teeth he doesn't easily let go! It is such persistence which has untied many knots and helped people through patient listening and counselling as he seeks to 'prepare people for heaven'.

This chapter seeks to paint some kind of picture of the three men behind the theology and to attempt an estimate of their influence. The various anecdotes selected are typical of their various characters. Their brother-in-law says, 'They are all different - intensely human, occasionally frustrating, but I have enjoyed immensely their friendship and the challenge of their thought, even if sometimes it goes way over my head.'

The Torrances have been widely appreciated, again perhaps sometimes more abroad than in Scotland, but they have also been widely criticised. Their theology has meant everything to some, but has been attacked by others. Did it present too much of a challenge, has the tide of secularism been flowing too strongly or was their presentation lacking? Whatever the reasons, right or wrong, for the widespread controversy or disagreement that their theology has caused it is to be hoped that they can be seen as each offering different insights and emphases, and as human. In each their theology flows from a simplicity of faith. While strongly intellectual it is never to be divorced from faith but understood out of it. In each of their differing ways they are endeavouring to be servants of the Triune God as they try to pass on the Gospel that they, in turn, have received. The passion comes from the heart of the Gospel - 'we love because he first loved us'.

For Further Reading

Thomas F. Torrance

Theological Science, London: Oxford, 1969
Belief in Science and in Christian Life (ed.), Edinburgh: Handsel, 1980
The Incarnation (ed.), Edinburgh: Handsel, 1981
The Ministry of Women, Edinburgh: Handsel, 1992 - booklet
The Trinitarian Faith, Edinburgh: T&T Clark, 1995
Space, Time and Resurrection, Edinburgh: T&T Clark, reprint 1998

James B. Torrance

John Duns Scotus in a Nutshell (with Roland Walls), Edinburgh: Handsel, 1992 - booklet
Intro. to fifth edition of *The Nature of the Atonement* by J. McLeod Campbell, Edinburgh: Handsel 1996; Grand Rapids: Eerdman's 1996; Victoria, Australia: BBS Publication No 12, 1996
Worship, Community, and the Triune God of Grace, Carlisle: Paternoster, 1996; Grand Rapids: Eerdman's, 1997

David W. Torrance

Witness of the Jews to God (ed.), Edinburgh: Handsel Press, 1982
God, Family, and Sexuality (ed.), Edinburgh: Handsel Press, 1997

Resources for Renewal
FROM PLC PUBLICATIONS

Standing Firm: Reclaiming Christian Faith in Times of Controversy
By Parker T. Williamson

Standing Firm is a riveting account of how the Nicene Creed emerged out of fourth-century controversies over the deity of Christ. With clarity and passion, Williamson traces our modern religious concerns to the past and finds hope and resolution for the future.

Thomas F. Torrance, professor emeritus of theology at Edinburgh, Scotland, calls *Standing Firm* "one of the most brilliant, refreshing and helpful books concerned with the heart and centre of the life and witness of the church that has happened in recent years."

An excellent resource for church study groups. Single copies: $12, plus shipping and handling.

I Believe …: The Apostles' Creed for the Third Millennium
By Robert P. Mills

Throughout two millennia Christians have affirmed their faith by voicing the bedrock principles of the Apostles' Creed. But repetition without reflection can dull the understanding of the timeless declarations that help frame the content of Christian confession.

In *I Believe … The Apostles' Creed for the Third Millennium*, Robert P. Mills underscores the biblical foundation for the Apostles' Creed and its powerful contemporary relevance.

I Believe … is presented in a format that is ideal for 26-week studies by church officers, Sunday school classes or other study groups.

Single copies: $5, plus shipping and handling.

Belonging to Christ:
Basic Biblical Truths for Discipleship
By Donna Phillips Munson

Belonging to Christ teaches the great doctrines of the Christian faith with life-changing, contemporary relevance. Young people survey classic Christian teachings and study the Scriptures to understand more fully how to live with a dynamic faith. In the process, they learn about the love of God, the Church, themselves and the joy that comes from knowing Christ. They are equipped not only to answer questions about discipleship, but also to proclaim and live those truths among their friends and family.

Involvement by parents, both in classes and home study, is a vital component of the curriculum. Many parents say their first understanding of the Church's classic doctrines came through *Belonging to Christ*.

Single copies: $18.75, plus shipping and handling.

Whom Alone We Worship and Serve:
What the Bible Teaches about God
By Robert P. Mills

This exciting 12-lesson Bible study blends first-rate scholarship, devotional insight and practical application. The text feeds the soul, fires the heart and sharpens the mind. *Whom Alone* interweaves the witness of Scripture, the insights of scholars from early church fathers to current evangelical commentators, and the historic Reformed perspective.

Single copies: $4.50, plus shipping and handling.

To order copies call toll-free: **1-800-368-0110**

Or place an order online at www.layman.org

PLC Publications • PO Box 2210 • Lenoir, NC 28645-2210